ANGELS

ANGELS

The Role of Celestial Guardians and Beings of Light

by
PAOLA GIOVETTI

translated by
Toby McCormick

SAMUEL WEISER, INC.

York Beach, Maine

First published in 1993 by
Samuel Weiser, Inc.
Box 612
York Beach, ME 03910

Translated from the Italian by Toby McCormick, Rome,
Italy.

Library of Congress Cataloging-in-Publication Data
Giovetti, Paola.
   [Angeli. English]
   Angels : the role of celestial guardians and
beings of light / by Paola Giovetti.
     p.   cm.
   Includes bibliographical references.
   1. Angels.   I. Title.
   BT966.2.G56 1993
   235'.3--dc20   92--44084
                                               CIP
ISBN 0-87728-779-1
BJ

Cover art is titled "Vallombrosa Altarpiece, detail of Angel
Musicians," by Pietro Perugino (c. 1445-1523), from the
Galleria dell'Accademia, Florence, Italy. Used by kind per-
mission from the Bridgeman Art Library, London.

Typeset in 12 point Palatino

Printed in the United States of America

The paper used in this publication meets the minimum
requirements of the American National Standard for Per-
manence of Paper for Printed Library Materials Z39.48-
1984.

Table of Contents

Foreword

A theologian recently defined angels as a "forgotten category." We do, indeed, talk more often and with increasing interest of devils and people possessed by them—or by demons, black masses, the casting of spells and exorcisms. Not so very long ago, angels played a natural and undisputed part in our religious thinking; but today not even theologians take much notice of them.[1] This is not surprising. In today's world many people are non-religious and averse to metaphysics, and it is hard enough to speak of God, let alone of such a lofty and fleeting subject as angels!

This does not, however, discredit the metaphysical reality of angels that has been authenticated by the scriptures. The fact that we do not speak, or speak very little about them does not make them non-existent. Angels appear in many religious traditions, always in the role of intermediaries between the human and divine realms. They date back to the Old Testament and earlier still, and have accompanied humanity through-out the centuries.

When, in 1781, a Spanish Mission was founded in California, it was called Los Angeles. When we speak today of this metropolis, the third largest in area and population in the United States, hardly anyone is aware that it was named after the angels. It would today be unthinkable even to name a single street after them. Once it was not like this, however. Our forebears felt themselves to be in the company of angels, built

---

[1] The journal *Prospettive nel Mondo* (March, 1989), edited by Gian Paolo Cresci, published the results of an opinion poll on the cult of Angels in Italy, from a sample of 1070 questionnaires. The results showed that only 8 percent of the compilers believed in guardian angels, and only 2 percent ask them for protection.

churches and chapels dedicated to them, and did their best to express in images their supernatural likenesses.

Despite the general indifference, voices are still heard now and then reminding us that angels exist. Sporadic voices, but none the less eloquent for being so. It seems that there are still some among us who have seen angels and been rescued or helped by them. Others have made investigations into them, and some have even had ineffable "angelic experiences."

Why should we not, then, collect these traditions and the evidence of witnesses? Offer them to the attention of readers who may very likely have more nostalgia for angels than curiosity about demons!

This is what I have tried to do. I do not, of course, claim to have made any definitive assertions. My intention was simply to present stories and events on which to meditate. These "angelic encounters" have given me, personally—in this epoch of the revival of devils—joy and serenity. I trust that anyone who cares to read to the end of this book will experience the same feelings.

—PAOLA GIOVETTI

PART
I

ANGELS
OF
HISTORY

Figure 1. Forgetful angel. Drawing by Paul Klee.

Chapter 1

Angels in Religious Tradition

In the prologue to Luigi Santucci's play *L'Angelo di Caino*, a white-clad and splendidly translucent angel addresses the audience with these—to use the appropriate adjective—winged words: "Oh ye baptized, lend me your ears. I am the angel. Who are the angels? Does anyone among you remember? . . . I can read your thoughts. No, not all these things, not only these things . . . You thought of your mother. And you of your dead child. And you others of a piece of music, a white image hung at the head of the bed. But it is right that you should know. You might not be able to stand our presence if you were to think of us as we really are, close to you at every instant. Whether you think of us or not, we are with you, oh ye baptized, in the precise and peremptory way God willed, forever and ever. With no distractions and no vacations!"[2]

In fact, the angels are close, always and at every instant, not only to the baptized, but to the peoples of all religions. In countless traditions they act as intermediaries between heaven and earth, as the messengers of God and guardians of humanity.

_____

[2]Luigi Santucci: *L'Angelo di Caino*, a play published in Italy. Translation is mine. Tr. note.

Although it is in the monotheistic religions that angels as we know them today prevail, we also find in other religions and mythologies supernatural figures performing the truly angelic role of guides, protectors, comforters, intermediate beings halfway between the sacred and the profane, heaven and earth, God and man. Guardian angels—angels of life and death.

If we study the very earliest beginnings of the peoples of Earth we find spirits of nature as well, as neutral as air and water, protectors of the manifestations of the natural world; and also demons who incarnate the principle of evil.

In the polytheistic religions, the line of demarcation between these supernatural beings and the divinity itself is often rather hazy; but it becomes clearer and more precise with the advent of monotheism.

The multiform evidence of the existence of an angelical world to be found in literature and religious history has led experts to come to conclusions that are not always concordant regarding the birth of the "angel" concept and its reciprocal influences on different peoples and religions. What does transpire, however, is the common experience that lies at the basis of all the traditions that have come down to us.

The earliest traces of the figure of an angel are to be found in the religion of the Assyrians and Babylonians, where each divinity had its heralds. These were winged figures that came down to earth from the sky and acted as messengers. The Babylonians also had the idea of divine protectors of each single individual; supernatural beings who interceded with the gods on our behalf, abandoned us when we misbehaved, and returned and pardoned us if we repented.

The Parsees believed in a spiritual world divided into two parts that rotated round two different and opposite poles, the principles of good and evil. The principle of good was surrounded by a class of divine beings called *Fravashi*, who were similar to the angels in many respects. Each individual had one of these beings to protect and defend him or her in the struggle against the demons.

We also find angelic and demoniacal beings in the Far Eastern traditions. They make up vast and complex cosmogonies. In India, for example, even today—thirty centuries after the Veda—the universe is conceived to be a hierarchy of powers of all kinds in perpetual action and venerated by the faithful. There is ample evidence of this in the extremely rich iconography that adorns Indian temples. Alongside the gods we find an indescribable multitude of secondary figures, angels and demons, nymphs and guardian spirits, airy divinities and earthly monsters. Hindu literature also abounds in descriptive scenes involving fairies and demons.

Buddhism and Brahmanism, which have spread also to Tibet, Java and Cambodia, also envisage numerous intermediary beings, some beneficent and friendly to people and others maleficent and hostile. In Burma and Pakistan people accept the existence of *nats*, guardian spirits who live alongside people and even sometimes inside them. Their number is infinite and their importance varies a great deal. Their presence, when felt, is generally beneficial, but requires propitiatory rites. There is also no shortage of maleficent *nats*.

To all these beings is attributed the different nature of the realities of life, which may be either positive or negative. It is in the Middle Eastern tradition, however, that we find a particular emphasis on the figure of the guardian angel.

Our word "angel" derives from the Greek αγγελos, meaning "messenger" and passed through Latin into the languages that are derived from it. To the Greeks, though, the term had a more limited meaning, standing for the divinities who protected the dead. Hermes was their leader, Artemis the goddess of the Underworld, and Zeus (called αγαθος αγγελος i.e., the "good angel") was the supreme deity.

In Greek mythology and especially in that mine of information and news that are the Homeric poems, we find divine figures with functions altogether similar to those of the angels of our own tradition. Athena, for example, in the first book of the Iliad, behaves toward Achilles in a manner that is very close to that of the sort of guardian angel we are used to. Only he can see her when she comes to give him advice as to how to combat Agamemnon. But Agamemnon, too, gets divine aid; Nestor appears to him in a dream, qualifying himself as a "messenger of Zeus" charged with bringing him certain suggestions. In book 24 it is Iris, the goddess of the rainbow, who is sent by Zeus as a messenger to comfort the aged King Priam as he weeps over the body of his dead son Hector.

In the Odyssey, Ulysses is several times rescued by the father of the gods through the intervention of Athena and the winged Hermes. It is Hermes who helps him free himself from the sorceries of the nymph Calypso by announcing to her that the gods have decreed that Ulysses must regain his long-desired freedom.

When he reaches the Pheacians, and the land of the Cyclops, Ulysses is aware of being guided by a god who has come to rescue him. When he finally lands on Ithaca and doubts whether he will be strong enough to overcome his numerous enemies, it is the face of Athena, once again, that encourages and assures him of final victory.

Just briefly to mention the Ancient Greek philosophers, we find numerous references in Plato to intermediary beings existing in heaven and on earth. One of these is Eros, the demigod of ancient myths who is sometimes quoted in the Homeric poems. Plato refers to the duties of Eros when he said that Eros was charged with the task of interpreting and presenting to the gods the things that come from people, and to people what the gods require—prayer, and offerings on the one hand, and acceptance of the orders and offerings on the other.

It is through the "demoniacal" element, understood here to mean supernatural and immortal, that—according to Plato—the art of the priests is manifested with reference to victims, dedications, prophecies, and magic. He said that God does not deal directly with people, and dialogue between the gods and humans is through intermediaries, both while they are awake and asleep. There are many demons and spirits, of all kinds, and one of them is Eros. Although the word "angel" does not yet appear, the role of these beings who exist halfway between the divine and the human is already clearly defined.

Socrates often referred to the interior voice that accompanied him throughout his life and which he called his *daimonion*—something between a guardian angel and a conscience. "It began in my early childhood—a sort of voice which comes to me; and when it comes it always dissuades me from what I am proposing to do, and never urges me on" (Apology 31d).[3]

---

[3]*Plato: The Last Days of Socrates (Euthyphro, The Apology, Crito, Phaedo)*, tr. Hush Tredennick (New York and London: Penguin Books, 1954), p. 64.

Many of the elements we have spoken of so far—in particular those that derive from Assyria and Babylon and the Parsees—are found in the Hebrew religion, which conceived One God, Javhè, who existed in heaven, surrounded by a court of angels, ministers, and messengers. Judaism and Christianity have in common the evidence of the Old Testament, and it is to this that we shall shortly refer.

But, before concentrating our attention on the sacred texts of our tradition, let us consider the significance of the presence of angels in the religion of Islam, which was influenced to a considerable extent by the Old Testament. The Ishmaelites, who considered themselves to be descendants of Ishmael, are the sect that recognizes the Aga Khan as their sovereign, on the basis of the event that is reported in chapter 21 of Genesis.

To summarize: Sarah conceived and miraculously bare Abraham a son Isaac in his old age. She then asked him to cast out his bondwoman Hagar in favor of this long-desired son, and disown Hagar's son Ishmael. Abraham was unwilling to do so, but God told him to hearken unto her voice, for his seed was to thrive in the descendants of Isaac, but that he would make a nation also of the son of the bondwoman.

Abraham therefore gave Hagar bread and a bottle of water, handed her child over to her and sent her away. She wandered in the wilderness of Beer-sheba until there was no more water in the bottle. Then God sent an angel: "And God heard the voice of the lad; and the angel of God called to Hagar out of heaven and said unto her. What aileth thee Hagar? fear not; for God hath heard the voice of the lad where he is. Arise, lift up the lad, and hold him in thine hand; for I will make him a great nation. And God opened her eyes, and she saw a well of water. . . . " (Genesis 21:17–19).[4]

Angels and archangels, in particular Michael and Gabriel, are often mentioned in the Koran. It is through the archangel Gabriel, who appears to him in a dream, that Mahomet receives his vocation (A.D. 610). The tradition also has it that Mahomet was accompanied by angels at his death. When he was about to die, his relatives had a vision: the room was filled with a host of angels who bathed it in a splendid light. The angel of death went up to Mahomet and asked permission to take his soul. Mahomet agreed, asking the angel only to perform his task rapidly.

We do not know from what source Mahomet obtained his knowledge of the Jewish and Christian traditions, but there is no doubt that he was influenced by them. The result is that Islamic angels play more or less the same role as those we find in the Scriptures. They are seated round the throne of Allah, from whose breath they were created, praising him and asking pardon for sinners, thus playing in full the role of intermediaries we know so well.

Proceeding in chronological order, we find an extensive and fascinating doctrine of angels in the works of the Muslim philosopher, poet, and theologian Avicenna (970–1037) who was born and lived in Persia. He envisaged a double cosmogony: invisible heavens joined to the visible astronomical and physical skies, and the angelical intelligences who originate the visible phenomena of the universe. He, too, often mentions Gabriel as the archangel of humanity and Michael as the messenger of the prophets.

---

[4]*The Revised King James Version of the Holy Bible* (Oxford: Oxford University Press). All biblical references in this book come from this version of the Bible.

Winged beings intermediating between heaven and earth are also found in the mystical texts of the Sufi, the visions of the shamans, the legends of the North American Indians as well as in Hinduism and Buddhism, as we have already seen.

We may claim without any fear of being mistaken that there is no earthly religious tradition that fails to take into account the role and functions of angels.

Angels in the Old Testament

There is no real established angelology in the Old Testament—no dogmatic system describing angels, their nature and relations with God and human beings. What we do find is evidence that God's relationship with us is through the agency of his messengers. The Jews of that time were firmly convinced that God made use of angels to rule the world and make history.

Angels therefore inhabit the intermediate steps on the ladder that leads up from the human being to God. To use the fine words of Giuseppe del Ton: "Nature does not proceed by leaps and bounds. From the protozoa to humanity there is an entire scale of beings, harmoniously graded in its variety of forms and operations, which makes us admire the infinite wisdom, and what we may call the creative imagination of God. Thus, to integrate the scheme of unity between ourselves and the Throne of the Divine Majesty, there are the Angels: pure spirits, shining intelligences, possessing vigorous wills. Furnaces of love and power, not destined—as human beings are—to take the form of corporeal organisms."[5]

---

[5]Giuseppe del Ton, *Verità su angeli e arcangeli* (Giardini ed., 1985). Translation is ours.

Already in Genesis we can see angels at work. "Therefore the LORD God sent him forth from the garden of Eden, to till the ground from whence he was taken. So he drove out the man; and he placed at the east of the garden of Eden Cherubims, and a flaming sword which turned every way, to keep the way of the tree of life" (Genesis 3:23, 24).

In chapter 16 we find the beginning of the story of Ishmael, to whom we already referred when considering Islam and the origin of the Ishmaelites. Sarah, who was childless, suggests to her husband Abraham that he should go in unto his bondwoman Hagar and seek to obtain his longed-for heir by her.

So Abraham lay with Hagar and she became pregnant. But from that moment the bondwoman despised her mistress, and when Sarah dealt harshly with her, Hagar fled from her face. Then we read: "And the angel of the LORD found her by a fountain of water in the wilderness . . . and . . . said unto her, Return to thy mistress, and submit thyself under her hands. . . . I will multiply thy seed exceedingly, that it shall not be numbered for multitude." The angel of the Lord then adds: "Behold, thou art with child, and shalt bear a son, and shalt call his name Ishmael; because the LORD hath heard thy affliction" (Genesis 16:7ff).

In chapter 18, Abraham is visited by three angels who announce, along with other things, that his wife Sarah, who was sterile and old (Abraham himself was already 100) would conceive and bear a son called Isaac. And when the Lord tempted Abraham by ordering him to sacrifice his son, it was an angel again who came to hold his hand: "And Abraham stretched forth his hand, and took the knife to slay his son. And the angel of the LORD called unto him out of Heaven, and said: Abraham, Abraham: and he said, Here am I. And he said,

Lay not thine hand upon the lad, neither do thou any thing unto him: for now I know that thou fearest God, seeing thou hast not witheld thy son, thine only son from me" (Genesis 22:10–12).

Later on we find Jacob's dream of the heavenly ladder: "And he dreamed, and behold a ladder set up on the earth, and the top of it reached to heaven; and behold the angels of God ascending and descending on it" (Genesis 28:12). Then there is Jacob wrestling with the angel (Genesis 32:25); and Moses and the "burning bush": "And the angel of the LORD appeared unto him in a flame of fire out of the midst of a bush" (Exodus 3:2).

In the book of Judges an angel announces another miraculous birth – that of the hero Samson. Before quoting the essentials of the biblical narrative it should be pointed out that the Israelites had done evil in the sight of the Lord, who delivered them into the hands of the Philistines for forty years. And it was Samson who was destined to liberate his people.

"There was a certain man . . . whose name was Manoah; and his wife was barren, and bare not. And the angel of the LORD appeared unto the woman, and said unto her, Behold now, thou art barren, and bearest not: but thou shalt conceive, and bear a son. . . . and he shall begin to deliver Israel out of the hand of the Philistines" (Judges 13:2–5).

The woman went to her husband and told him that she had seen a man with a countenance like the countenance of an angel of God who announced that she was about to be pregnant. Then Manoah prayed to the Lord that he send again his angel. And the angel did return and gave counsel to the woman and advised Manoah to sacrifice a kid to celebrate the event. And another prodigy took place: ". . . when the flame [that was burning the kid] went up toward heaven from off the altar? . . . the angel of the LORD ascended in the flame of the altar" (Judges 13:20).

From then on the angel did not appear again to Manoah or his wife, but what he had announced came to pass. It is clearly stated that the angel had a human countenance, but was of such majesty and transfigured by such a powerful light that Manoah's wife guessed his true nature. Manoah, though, remained unconvinced of the angelic nature of his visitor until he saw him ascend to heaven in the flame.

It was an angel, too, who comforted the prophet Elijah when: ". . . he went . . . a day's journey into the wilderness, and came and sat down under a juniper tree: and he requested for himself that he might die; and said, It is enough; now, O LORD, take away my life; for I am not better than my fathers." He then lay down and slept under the juniper, and an angel touched him and said to him, "Arise and eat! And he looked and, behold, and there was a cake baked on the coals, and a cruse of water at his head. And he did eat and drink, and laid him down again. And the angel of the LORD came again a second time, and touched him and said: Arise and eat; because the journey is too great for thee. And he arose, and did eat and drink, and went in the strength of that meat forty days and forty nights . . ." (I Kings 19:4–8).

In the book of Isaiah we read about the consecration of Isaiah as a prophet: "In the year that king Uzziah died I saw also the Lord sitting upon a throne, high and lifted up, and his train filled the temple. Above it stood the seraphims: each one had six wings; with twain he covered his face, and with twain he covered his feet, and with twain he did fly. And one cried unto another, and said, Holy, holy, holy, is the LORD of hosts: the whole earth is full of his glory. And the posts of the door moved at the voice of him that cried, and the house was filled with smoke. Then said I, Woe is me! for I am undone; because I am a man of unclean lips, and I dwell in the midst of a people of unclean lips: for mine eyes have seen the King, the LORD of hosts. Then flew one of the seraphims unto me, having a live coal in his hand, which he had taken with a tong from off the altar: And he laid it upon my mouth, and said Lo, this hath touched thy lips; and thine iniquity is taken away, and thy sin purged" (Isaiah 6:1-7).

The book of Daniel is particularly stimulating in its references to angels. The three young men who had refused to fall down and worship king Nebuchadnezzar were cast into the burning fiery furnace from which they were rescued by the Lord: ". . . the king . . . said unto his counsellors, Did we not cast three men bound into the midst of the fire? . . . Lo, I see four men loose, walking in the midst of the fire, and they have no hurt; and the form of the fourth is like the Son of God." The king then had the three come forth from the fire and everyone could see that no hair of their heads was singed, and Nebuchadnezzar said, "Blessed be the LORD God of Shadrach, Meshach, and Abednego who hath sent his angel and delivered his servants that trusted in him, and have changed the king's word, and yielded their bodies, that they might not serve nor worship any god except their own God" (Daniel 3:24-28).

Later on, the king had Daniel cast into the den of lions and left him there all night long. On the following morning Nebuchadnezzar went to the den and asked Daniel if his Lord had come to his aid, and Daniel replied "My God hath sent his angel, and hath shut the lions' mouths, that they have not hurt me" (Daniel 6:22).

It is in the book of Daniel that, for the first time, there is mention of an angel named Gabriel. It is he who interprets to Daniel a vision he has had: "And it came to pass, when I, even I Daniel, had seen the vision, and sought for the meaning, then, behold, there stood before me as the appearance of a man. And I heard a man's voice . . . which called, and said Gabriel, make this man to understand the vision. So he came near where I stood: and when he came, I was afraid, and fell upon my face" (Daniel 8:15–17).

Later on we also find the name of the archangel Michael: "Then I lifted up mine eyes, and looked, and behold a certain man clothed in linen, whose loins were girded with fine gold of Uphaz. His body also was like the beryl, and his face as the appearance of lightning, and his eyes as lamps of fire, and his arms and his feet like in colour to polished brass, and the voice of his words like the voice of a multitude" (Daniel 10:5,6). "Then he said unto me. . . . The prince of the kingdom of Persia withstood me one and twenty days: but lo, Michael, one of the chief princes, came to help me. . . . Now I am come to make thee understand what shall befall thy people in the latter days" (Daniel 10:12–14).

Lastly, the young Tobias is accompanied and protected by the archangel Raphael on his dangerous voyage: "Tobias went out in search of one who knew the road so that he might accompany him into the land of the Medes. He went out and saw before him the Angel Raphael, without in the least suspecting that this was an angel of God" (Tobias 5:4). The angel showed Tobias that he knew those lands very well and accompanied him on his journey. Before leaving he consoled the mother of Tobias who was weeping, assuring her that her son would return safe and sound because he was to be guided by an angel of God.

Thus all three archangels appear in the Old Testament and are called by name.

The angels in the Old Testament have a human aspect, eat and drink like humans and do not always have wings. In his *Dictionaire Philosophique*, Voltaire says of the corporeality of the Old Testament angels: "These angels were corporeal; they had wings on their shoulders, as the Gentiles imagined Mercury to have them on his feet; and they sometimes hid their wings under their clothing. And how could they not be corporeal, since they drank and ate, and if the inhabitants of Sodom tried to perform acts of pederasty on the angels who appeared to Lot? " He also says that it is not precisely known where the angels are, in the air, in the void or on the planets; and he mentions that God has willed that we should not be informed of this.[6]

The Book of Enoch

The *Book of Enoch* is part of the so-called apochryphal gospels, a name that was given by the early Church to writings that came from the environment of the Jews and were therefore connected with the history of the origins of Christianity, but were not accepted as part of the canon. As time passed they were forgotten or lost, only to have been rediscovered relatively recently. The *Book of Enoch*, for example, was found at the end of the 18th century in an Ethiopic manuscript.[7]

It is a book that was judged to be of considerable importance during the first centuries of the Church's existence, and it is quoted in the New Testament as belonging to the Scriptures. In the Epistle of Jude

---

[6]Translation is mine.

[7]R. H. Charles, *Book of Enoch* (Oxford: Clarendon Press, 1912). R. H. Charles translated the Ethiopic text.

(14–15), for example, we read: "And Enoch also, the seventh from Adam, prophesied of these, saying, Behold the Lord cometh with ten thousands of his saints, to execute judgment upon all, and to convince all that are ungodly among them of all their ungodly deeds . . . and of all their hard speeches which ungodly sinners have spoken against him."

There is also a close literary and ideological connection between the New Testament and the Book of Enoch, which the Pharisees, at a certain point, removed from the canon, although the Church Fathers continued to quote from it.

To anyone who studies angels, this book is a mine of information. We may even claim that it provides a genuine angelology, i.e., a doctrine of angels. From the very beginning, the Book refers to winged spirits who are divine messengers by whom the author states that he was informed of everything he writes: "the Angels showed me, and from them I heard everything, and from them I understood as I saw, but not for this generation, but for a remote one which is to come."[8]

The most important chapter is the sixth, which is also known as the Book of Vigilantes and should be considered as the earliest source for the Jewish conception of the fall of the angels.[9] Here is what it says:

"And it came to pass when the children of men had multiplied that in those days were born unto them beautiful and comely daughters. And the angels, the children of the heaven, saw and lusted after them, and said to one another: 'Come let us choose us wives from among the children of men and beget us children.' And

[8]Check the New English translation of Genesis 6:4, and we will certainly discuss the fall of the "Sons of God," and they don't mean the sons of Adam. Publisher's note.
[9]R. H. Charles, *Book of Enoch* (Oxford: Clarendon Press, 1912), 1: 2.

Semjaza, who was their leader, said unto them: 'I fear ye will not indeed agree to do this deed, and I alone shall have to pay the penalty of a great sin.' And they all answered him and said: 'Let us all swear an oath and bind ourselves by mutual imprecations not to abandon this plan but to do this thing.' Then sware they all together and bound themselves by mutual imprecations upon it. And they were in all two hundred. . . .'"[10]

There follows a long list of names, including those of Asael, Batarel, Ananel, Ezekiel and Daniel. The text then continues: "And . . . they took unto themselves wives, and each chose for himself one, and they began to go in unto them and to defile themselves with them, and they taught them charms and enchantments, and the cutting of roots, and made them acquainted with plants. And they became pregnant and they bare great giants, whose height was three thousand ells. Who consumed all the acquisitions of men. And when men could no longer sustain them, the giants turned against them and devoured mankind. And they began to sin against birds, and beasts, and reptiles, and fish, and to devour one another's flesh, and drink the blood. Then the earth laid accusation against the lawless ones.[11]

Thus evil came to pass on earth with the fall of the children of God, who taught men—we read further in Enoch—to forge for themselves arms and armor plating, to know the value of gold and precious stones, to practice magic and astrology and to fight against one another. And the fallen angels taught the women to wear makeup and jewelry and paint their eyebrows. And the consequence was that their knowledge increased and they knew wars, impurities and sin.

---

[10]R. H. Charles, *Book of Enoch* (Oxford: Clarendon Press, 1912), 6: 13–17.
[11]*Book of Enoch*, 7: 18.

Equally of interest regarding the angels is another Apocryphal text, *The Book of Jubilees*,[12] which is also known as the "little Genesis" as it tells of the history of the world from the creation to the time when Moses, on Mount Sinai, received the Tables of the Law from the Lord.

While there is no mention in the Old Testament of the creation of the angels, *The Book of Jubilees* refers expressly to this, and states that among the works of God on the first day of the creation was that of the spirits and angels. We can read that *angelus faceiei*—i.e., the angel who was always at the side of the Lord—explained the process of the creation to Moses:

And the angel of the presence spake to Moses according to the word of the Lord, saying: "Write the complete history of the creation, how in six days the Lord God finished all His works and all that He created, and kept Sabbath on the seventh day and hallowed it for all ages, and appointed it as a sign for all His works. For on the first day He created the heavens which are above and the earth and the waters and all the spirits which serve before Him—the angels of the presence, and the angels of sanctification, and the angels [of the spirit of fire and the angels] of the spirit of the winds, and the angels of the spirit of the clouds, and of darkness, and of snow and of hail and of hoar frost, and the angels of the voices and of the thunder and of the lightning, and the angels of the spirits of cold and of heat, and of winter and of spring and of autumn and of summer, and of all the spirits of His creatures which are in the heavens and on the earth, (He created) the abysses and the darkness, eventide (and night), and the light,

---

[12]*The Book of Jubilees* or *The Little Genesis*, tr. R. H. Charles (London: Society for Promoting Christian Knowledge, 1917).

dawn and day, which He hath prepared in the knowledge of His heart."[13]

On the following days the Lord fashioned the fir-
mament, separated the land from the waters, created
the sun, moon and stars, the plants, the animals and
man, as it says in Genesis. The creation of the angels on
the first day, as reported in *The Book of Jubilees* is a new
element, of which the canonical books do not speak.
This is certainly an interesting factor in our study.

Angels in the New Testament

The interventions of angels in the New Testament are
even more numerous than in the Old, and have
inspired an infinity of paintings and sculptures.

We find the first angelical experience in Luke
(1:11–12) who says that one day when the priest Zacharias, who was well striken in years, as was his wife
Elizabeth who was also barren, was in the temple: ". . .
there appeared unto him an angel of the Lord standing
on the right side of the altar of incense. And when
Zacharias saw him, he was troubled, and fear fell upon
him." The well-known story goes that the angel
announced to Zacharias that his wife would bear a son
who was to be called John. Because Zacharias doubted,
the angel rendered him dumb and unable to speak until
the day of the birth of his son. This announcement is
very similar to those made by the angel to Abraham and
Sarah and Manoah and his wife in the Old Testament—
a motive that recurs in the Scriptures on a number of
occasions.

The most joyful announcement by an angel is, of
course, that made to Mary. Luke continues: "And in the

---

[13]*The Book of Jubilees*, tr. R. H. Charles (London: Society for Promoting
Christian Knowledge, 1917), pp. 40, 41.

sixth month [of Elizabeth's pregnancy] the angel Gabriel was sent from God unto a city of Galilee, named Nazareth. To a virgin espoused to a man whose name was Joseph, of the house of David; and the virgin's name was Mary. And the angel came in unto her, and said, Hail, thou that art highly favoured, the Lord is with thee: blessed art thou among women." And she was troubled by these words and wondered what sort of salutation that was. "And the angel said unto her, Fear not Mary: for thou hast found favour with God. And behold, thou shalt conceive in thy womb, and bring forth a son, and shalt call his name JESUS . . . " (Luke 1:26ff).

Matthew (1:19ff) relates that when Mary became pregnant: "Joseph her husband, being a just man, and not willing to make her a publick example, was minded to put her away privily. But while he thought on these things, behold, the angel of the Lord appeared unto him in a dream saying, Joseph, thou son of David, fear not to take unto thee Mary thy wife; for that which is conceived in her is of the Holy Ghost." The angel then reminded Joseph of the prophesy of Isaiah: "A virgin shall conceive, and bear a son . . . " Matthew continues: "Then Joseph being raised from sleep did as the angel of the Lord had bidden him, and took unto him his wife . . . " (Matthew 1:19–24).

The birth of Jesus is announced to the shepherds by angels: "And there were in the same country shepherds abiding in the field, keeping watch over their flock by night. And, lo, the angel of the Lord came upon them, and the glory of the Lord shone round about them: and they were sore afraid. And the angel said unto them, Fear not: for, behold, I bring you good tidings of great joy, which shall be to all people . . . for unto you is born . . . a Saviour" (Luke 2:8ff). When Jesus was circumcised, Luke again speaks of the angel: "And when eight days were accomplished for the circumcising of the child, his name was called JESUS, which was so named of the angel before he was conceived in the womb" (Luke 2:21).

Matthew says that when Herod ordered the massacre of the innocents, an angel appeared to Joseph in a dream saying: "Arise, and take the young child and his mother, and flee into Egypt, and be thou there until I bring thee word: for Herod will seek the young child to destroy him (Matthew 2:13). After the danger had passed the angel returned: "When Herod was dead, behold, an angel of the Lord appeareth in a dream to Joseph in Egypt, saying, Arise and take the young child and his mother, and go into the land of Israel: for they are dead which sought the young child's life" (Matthew 2:19–20).

When Jesus fasted for 40 days before beginning his teaching and preaching in Galilee and was tempted by the devil, it was the angels who came: "Then the devil leaveth him, and, behold, angels came and ministered unto him" (Matthew 4:11).

Throughout his life, Jesus was constantly accompanied by angels and he often referred to them. It is written, for example, in the parable of the grain of mustard seed: "The Son of man shall send forth his angels, and they shall gather out of his kingdom all things that offend, and them which do iniquity; And shall cast them into a furnace of fire" (Matthew 13:41–42). Later on: "The Son of man shall come in the glory of his Father with his angels; and then he shall reward every man according to his works" (Matthew 16:27).

There is another reference to angels in the parable of the lost piece of silver: "Likewise, I say unto you, there is joy in the presence of the angels of God over one sinner that repenteth" (Luke 15:10).

Luke (16:22) also speaks of angels receiving the soul of a dead man: "And it came to pass, that the beggar died, and was carried by the angels into Abraham's bosom: the rich man also died, and was buried." Matthew (18:10) speaks of angels in heaven: "for I say unto you, That in heaven their angels do always behold the face of my Father which is in heaven."

The resurrection of Jesus is a veritable apotheosis of angels: "And, behold, there was a great earthquake: for the angel of the Lord descended from heaven, and came and rolled back the stone from the door and sat upon it. . . . and his raiment white as snow; And for fear of him the keepers did shake, and became as dead men. And the angel answered and said unto the women; Fear not ye: for I know that ye seek Jesus which was crucified. He is not here: for he is risen, as he said" (Matthew 28:2-6). And again: "And entering into the sepulchre, they saw a young man sitting on the right side, clothed in a long white garment; and they were affrighted" (Mark 16:5), or "And they found the stone rolled away from the sepulchre. And they entered in, and found not the body of the Lord Jesus. And it came to pass, as they were much perplexed thereabout, behold, two men stood by them in shining garments . . ." (Luke 24:2-4).

John (20:12) reports the same event as follows: "And seeth two angels in white sitting, the one at the head, and the other at the feet, where the body of Jesus had lain."

In the Acts of the Apostles (1:10-11) the story is told of the ascension of Jesus into heaven: "And while they looked stedfastly toward heaven as he went up, behold, two men stood by them in white apparel; Which also said . . . why stand ye gazing up into heaven? This same Jesus, which is taken up from you into heaven, shall so come in like manner as ye have seen him go into heaven."

There are numerous other mentions of angels in the Acts of the Apostles, for example when Peter is released from prison by an angel: "And when Herod would have brought him forth, the same night Peter was sleeping between two soldiers, bound with two chains: and the keepers before the door kept the prison. And, behold, the angel of the Lord came upon him, and a light shined in the prison: and he smote Peter on the side, and raised him up saying, Arise up quickly. And his chains fell off from his hands. And the angel said unto him, Gird thyself and bind on thy sandals. . . . And he went out, and followed him; and wist not that it was true which was done by the angel; but thought he saw a vision" (Acts 12:6–9).

It was an angel who sent Philip to convert the Ethiopians (Acts 8:26) "And the angel of the Lord spake unto Philip, saying, Arise, and go toward the south unto the way that goeth down from Jerusalem unto Gaza." The angel of death appears again at the death of Herod: "And immediately the angel of the Lord smote him, because he gave not God the glory; and he was eaten of worms" (Acts 12:23).

When Paul was about to journey to Rome, he exhorted his companions regaling them with the vision he had seen: "For there stood by me this night the angel of God, whose I am, and whom I serve. Saying, fear not, Paul; thou must be brought before Caesar; and, lo, God hath given thee all them that sail with thee" (Acts 27:23–24).

In his First Epistle to the Corinthians, Paul again refers to the angels when he says, (13:1): "Though I

Plate 1. According to tradition, angels have no previous conscious awareness of the incarnation, passion, and death of Jesus Christ. To them every aspect of his life and death is as wonderful and astonishing as it is to us human beings. This is perfectly expressed in Giotto's fresco in the Scrovegni Chapel at Padua, a detail of which is reproduced here. The painting is a Crucifixion in which the despair of the angels, seen flying round the cross like demented swallows, expresses the whole tragedy of the event.

Plate 2. The subject of the Annunciation has always been a favorite for artists. This version, sculptured in stone, dates to the first half of the 14th century and is in the Collegiate Church of Notre-Dame at Ecouis.

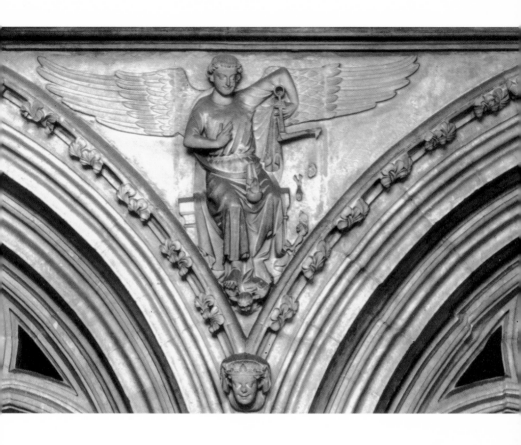

Plate 3. A representation in stone of a seated angel. The refined work of an unknown artist seems to have been inspired by the metalworkers' technique, especially in the soft and deep folds of the clothing. It was created between 1270 and 1280 and is in a corbel of the choir of Lincoln Cathedral in England.

Plate 4. The Egyptian goddess Isis, a virgin-mother protectress, is represented here as an angel whose huge many-colored wings embrace everything. The angel motif is found in all religious cultures and traditions, even before the advent of Christianity.

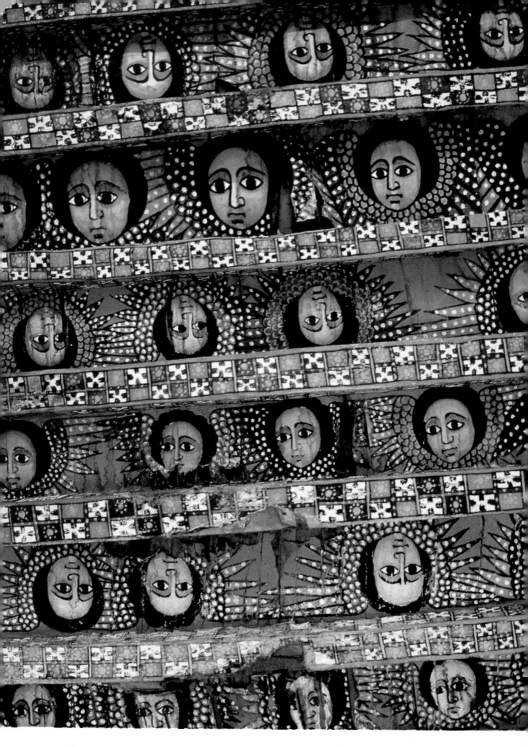

Plate 5. These faces, which adorn the ceiling of the Church of Debre Berhari in Ethiopia, are arranged to represent the different levels of reality, ascending as if on the steps of a ladder ever higher until they reach the First Principle which is beyond reality. An angel is encountered at each of these steps, the guardian, protector, and expression of each higher interior experience.

Plate 6. The "Dance of Bugaku" (1652–1724), a detail of a painting by Hanabusa Itcho. We do not know whether the winged intermediary between heaven and earth originated in ancient Japan or was borrowed from another source. In either case, this angelical figure is a powerful archetype of human experience, and appears spontaneously in all the cultures both East and West.

Plate 7. The fundamental task of angels is to act as messengers, intermediaries between the gods and men. This function is found in all the religious traditions. Here is a detail from a Mughal illuminated manuscript, and a detail of the "Annunciation" by Melozzo da Forlì.

Plate 8. A Christian mandala: the German mystic Hildegard of Bingen had a vision in which she saw God surrounded by nine choirs of angels corresponding to the hierarchies of spiritual beings in which He is manifest. God himself appears as a luminous disc in the center; the divinity is represented only as a brilliant light. One of the illuminations in Hildegard's breviary, 12th century.

Plate 9 (opposite). Lucifer is a fallen angel, a "blinded" creature as the Pope has called him. He tries to win the soul of those who die and bring them to hell. Here, the top part shows the archangel Michael at heaven's gate disputing with the Devil for the soul of someone. His good deeds are being weighed against his bad. The Devil and his attendants are up to their tricks to get the balance to come down on their side. An angel hands a soul, judged favorably, to St. Peter. Below, the souls of the damned have arrived in hell and are being tortured with fire. An altarpiece in the church of San Miguel at Suriguerola, Spain, 13th century.

32

Plate 10. Daniel, in the Lion's Den, is protected by a guardian angel. In both the Old and New Testament, angels are mentioned hundreds of times, often intervening deliberately to protect or save someone, as here Daniel. This representation dates to the eighth century and is by the Spanish monk Beatus and illustrates his commentary on the *Book of Revelations*.

34

Plate 11. The "Last Trump." The souls of the dead emerge from their tombs and dance with joy at the sound of the trumpeting angels. A pericope of Henry II, 11th century.

Plate 12. Gianfilippo Usellini: "The Great Battle," 1950. Tempera on canvas owned by Signora Camilla Ciceri, Milan. Usellini is an important 20th-century Italian painter, influenced by the 15th-century school. He produces work that is often ironical and of a primitive candor, treating serious and solemn subjects with a carefree grace that is extremely modern.

Plate 13. The Archangel Michael by Sansovino (1507), preserved in the Basilica of St. Michael on Monte San Michele in the Gargano Peninsula. The Archangel is represented in the attitude of a victorious warrior, trampling underfoot his adversary, a repugnant monster. According to the tradition, the Archangel Michael appeared at Gargano on several occasions between the years 490 and 1656. He showed the people a cave, sacred to him, in which his image is still venerated.

Plate 14. According to a very ancient tradition, the Holy House, venerated at Loreto inside the great Basilica, is the one in which the most miraculous event in the history of Christianity took place—the Annunciation to Mary. The house is supposed to have been brought to Loreto on the wings of angels. The faithful still believe this.

Plate 15 (opposite). These 16th-century murals, preserved in the crypt of the Cathedral at Bayeux in France, show angels engaged in the most poetic occupation attributed to them—that of musicians.

Plate 16. Santa Francesca Romana, the favorite Saint of the Roman people, lived from 1384 to 1440. She was accompanied by angels throughout her life, as represented by the frescoes of Antoniazzo Romano in the Chapel of the Monastery of Tor de'Specchi. Represented here is the boy angel that the Saint constantly saw at her side.

40

speak with the tongues of men and of angels, and have not charity, I am become as sounding brass, or a tinkling cymbal."

Lastly, we read in the Revelation (22:8): "And I John, saw these things, and when I had heard and seen, I fell down to worship before the feet of the angel which showed me these things." In this book, one angel shows John the images he describes, and another invites him to write of the things he has seen.

• • •

The Scriptures present no definite doctrine of the angels, but confront us directly with the fact of their existence. When were the angels created? In the Book of Job (38:7) we find expressions that lead us to believe that they were joyful and full of life before God proceeded to the creation of the material world: "When the morning stars sang together, and all the sons of God shouted for joy." In the apocryphal Book of Jubilees it is affirmed, as we have seen, that the angels were created by the Lord on the first day.

Nothing specific is said in the Scriptures about the nature of the angels or their exact relationship to God and people. From the numerous references made, however, it can be seen that God achieves a relationship with us through the angels, his messengers.

The angels we meet in the Bible are of a spiritual nature, but can also take on a physical form and make themselves visible and audible, appear and disappear. Yet they seem to be ageless, sexless, and immune from illness: "For in the resurrection they neither marry, nor are given in marriage, but are as the angels of God in heaven" as we can read in Matthew (22:30). Which leads us to think that they have more enjoyable things to do than having sex. We shall see, in the chapter on the Swedish clairvoyant Emanuel Swedenborg, what these occupations may be.

In the Old and New Testaments the angels are mentioned about three hundred times overall. We can read that there are myriads and myriads of them. David says that there are twenty thousand of them (Psalm 68:17). In Deuteronomy (33:2) ten thousand angels are seen to descend on Mount Sinai to confirm the presence of God when Moses is given the tables of the Law.

The angels, as we can surmise from reading the Bible, were created by God equal to people. Among their other duties they were set on guard at the entrance to Eden (Genesis 3:24). They thus became celestial sentinels charged to prevent us from returning to the garden from which the Lord had banished us.

As well as acting as messengers mediating between God and people, and custodians of the Garden of Eden, the angels, as is referred to briefly in the Old Testament, also had the task of protecting people. We find these words in Psalm (91:11–12):

> For he shall give his angels charge over thee,
>   to keep thee in all thy ways.
> They shall bear thee up in their hands,
> lest thou dash thy foot against a stone.

Even today the Roman Catholic Church still teaches that each of us has a guardian angel, and celebrates a feast day to them on October 2nd, with an appropriate ecclesiastical liturgy.

"The frailty of human nature, ephemeral and uncertain in the course of the terrestrial pilgrimage," says Giuseppe del Ton, one of the greatest living angelologists, "and the sublimity of his being destined to life in the heavens without limitation and endlessly blessed, required that a Spirit should be given to the soul to surround and protect it."[14]

In any case, St. Paul has this to say with reference to the guardianship of angels over people: "Are they not all ministering spirits, sent forth to minister for them who shall be heirs of salvation?" (Hebrews 1:14).

The same applies to the powers. Angels have greater powers than we do, but are not omnipotent. One single angel was enough to smite the firstborn in Egypt, and to close the mouths of the lions that threatened Daniel, yet they are subservient to the Lord: "Bless the Lord, ye his angels, that excel in strength, that do his commandments, hearkening unto the voice of his word" (Psalm 103:20).

The Bible also refers to the angelic hierarchies and speaks of angels, archangels, seraphim, cherubim, and other ranks, without actually presenting a structured *corpus* of information on the subject. In the first century of the Christian era, however, there lived someone who has provided us with a detailed description of the celestial hierarchies and codified very early traditions handed down by the Church Fathers. He was Dionysius the Areopagite, who will be the subject of the following chapter.

---

[14]Giuseppe del Ton, *Verità su angeli e arcangeli* (Giardini ed., 1985).

Figure 2. A seraph and two fiery ophanim. Sixth century bronze mirror.

Chapter 2

Celestial Hierarchies

The most authoritative source for our knowledge of Christian angelology is a Dionysius who is often confused with the biblical figure converted by St. Paul, but more correctly known as the Pseudo-Dionysius the Areopagite. His treatises *Celestial Hierarchies*, *On the Ecclesiastical Hierarchy*, *The Divine Names*, and his *Ten Letters* form a corpus that earned the esteem of a number of Popes including Gregory the Great of St. Thomas, the Scholastica, Dante and St. John of the Cross.

He was probably an Armenian monk who assumed the name of the Dionysius converted by St. Paul who is said to have witnessed at Heliopolis the eclipse of the sun at the moment of Christ's death, and attended the burial of the Virgin Mary with the apostles.

The *Celestial Hierarchies*, which provides valuable evidence of Western mysticism and the origins of Christianity, is the best known and appreciated text on Christian angelology. It collects and codifies the time-honored wisdom handed down by the Church Fathers, who for centuries represented the peak of Christian spirituality. This treatise has a great deal to say about the most blessed angelical hierarchies in which the

Father generously manifested His light and through which we can raise ourselves to His absolute splendor.[1]

It is stated in this text, for example, that those who belong to the hierarchies are like translucent mirrors and are able to receive the ray of Light of the Divine Principle, holily filled with the splendor due them, and in their turn resplendent to those that follow them. And he also says that when we speak of a hierarchy, we mean a holy order, an image of the beauty of the divine Principle. The hierarchy has a sacred function—to bring to consciousness the mysteries of its own illumination. It tends to become assimilated into its own Principle—becoming actually "a collaborator of God"—and demonstrating how it achieves this divine activity. He goes on to say that the celestial hierarchies participate in the divine Principle to a greater extent than humans can, and the illumination of the divine Principle is attained first in them, and is transmitted to us as superior revelations.

Getting down to specific detail, Dionysius said "I see[2] that the Angels, too, were first initiated into the divine mystery of Jesus in His love for man, and through them the gift of that knowledge was bestowed upon us: for the divine Gabriel announced to Zachariah the high-priest that the son who should be born to him through Divine Grace, when he was bereft of hope, would be a prophet of that Jesus who would manifest the union of the human and divine natures through the ordinance of the Good Law for the salvation of the world; and he revealed to Mary how of her should be born the Divine Mystery of the ineffable Incarnation of God." Another Angel taught Joseph that the divine

---

[1]Dionysius the Areopagite, *The Mystical Theology and The Celestial Hierarchies* (Godalmins, Surrey, UK: The Shrine of Wisdom, 1949).
[2]Dionysius clearly had visions which confirmed the biblical narrative.

promise made to his forefather David should be per-fectly fulfilled.[3]

Dionysius also says that the loftiest illuminations of the *Loghia*[4] now tell him that Jesus, himself, the super-essential head of the celestial entities came down to humanity, and submitted himself to the will of God the Father that was transmitted through the Angels. All this was revealed to us of the priestly traditions con-cerning the Angel that comforted Jesus. This same Jesus, having entered the order of revealers through his beneficent work of salvation, was proclaimed an Angel of Great Counsel.[5]

Regarding the real celestial hierarchies, Dionysius stated that only their divine initiatory Principle can know them exactly. It is not possible for human beings to know the celestial mysteries. Therefore we shall say nothing that comes only from ourselves, but shall expound, as far as we are able, those celestial visions that were contemplated by the saints who were aware of the Divine and to whom we have been initiated.

There are nine celestial orders, subdivided into three major orders: the first is that which is always in the presence of God and includes the holy Thrones and their courts with many eyes and many wings, i.e., the Cherubim and Seraphim. The second order includes the Powers, Dominions, and Virtues; the third the Angels, Archangels, and Principalities.

Each name of the celestial Intelligences is an indica-tion of its divine nature. Dionysius explained that the

---

[3]Dionysius the Areopagite, *The Celestial Hierarchies* (Godalmins, Surrey, UK: The Shrine of Wisdom, 1949), p. 34.
[4]By this term is meant what God had pronounced in the course of time and handed down in the sacred texts.
[5]Dionysius the Areopagite, *The Celestial Hierarchies*, (Godalmins, Surrey, UK: The Shrine of Wisdom, 1949), pp. 34, 35.

holy name of the Seraphim means both "those that burn" and "those that warm," and that of the Cherubim "fullness of knowledge" or "effusion of wisdom." The term "thrones" is used to indicate proximity to the Divine throne. They are the loftiest of beings who are seated next to God and receive directly and immediately from Him Divine perfection and awareness.

To explain the reason for the names given to the Seraphim and Cherubim, Dionysius claims that the Seraphim are in continuous and eternal revolution round the divine reality; the heat, the ardor and the capacity to render like unto themselves their subordinates, elevates them. Their cathartic power is like unto lightning, a luminous and resplendent nature that is never hidden and cannot be extinguished, avoiding every abode of dismal darkness. The name Cherubim tells us that they had the power to know and contemplate the Divinity, and the capacity to receive the gift of the utmost light, meditating on the dignity of the divine Principle in its original power, be filled with the gift of wisdom and communicate it, without envy, to those of the second order. As for the Thrones, these were very lofty and sublime spirits and their name tells us that they transcend in purity every vile inclination, ascending toward the summit in a manner that is extraterrestrial. They withdraw steadfastly from every lowly action, seated as they are firmly and legitimately around Him who is indeed the Most High, gleaning what descends from the Divine principle.

We now take a brief look at the intermediary order—the celestial Intelligences, known as Powers, Virtues, and Dominions—whose names reveal their characteristics. Dionysius said that the revealing name of the holy Dominions is indicative of their power to elevate themselves, liberated from all inferior yieldings.

They absolutely never abase themselves to any discordant or tyrannical reality, and enter into communication with the eternal divinity of the Principle of Dominion. The holy Virtues have a name that signifies a firm and intrepid courage in all activities. This is a courage that never tires of welcoming the illumination granted by the divine Principle and is potentially straining to attain imitation of God. The holy Powers is a name that shows they are at the same level as that of the divine Dominions and, with the Virtues, share a disposition that is most harmonious and has power and intelligence that elevates, with a goodness that is subordinate to the divine reality, and tends to become assimilated to the Principle of Power, the source of all power, and which radiates It, as far as possible, to the Angels.

The Angels possess the ability to become messengers and are the closest to us. The name Angel is more appropriate to them than that of the previous orders, since their hierarchy deals with that which is most manifest and, what is more, with the things of this world. This is why the Divine Wisdom has entrusted our hierarchy to the Angels, and nominated Michael as the prince of the Jewish people, calling on the other Angels to preside over the various peoples. Indeed, the Most High established the boundaries of the nations according to the number of the Angels of God.

In summarizing the tasks and duties of the celestial hierarchies, Dionysius affirms that the celestial Intelligences are all revealers and messengers of those that precede them. The most worthy are of God—who moves them—while the others, according to their strength, are of the entities that are moved by God. The superessential harmony of all things has provided for the regular elevation and holy harmonious disposition of each rational and intelligent being, and arranged each hierarchy into holy orders. We can see that the whole hierarchy is divided into primary, intermediary and tertiary powers. Yet the truth is that He has also subdivided each order according to the same divine relationships. Therefore those who have knowledge of the Divine declare that the same most high Seraphim "cry one unto another,"[6] thus demonstrating that it is they who first transmitted to the others their knowledge of the Divine.

Lastly, Dionysius pays attention to the number of the celestial intelligences and, in an apotheosis of great beauty, tells us that there is another thing that merits intelligent consideration: the tradition of the *Loghia* says of the Angels that they are "a thousand thousands" and "ten-thousand times ten thousand"[7]—repeating for this purpose and multiplying the highest numbers we use—with the intention of clearly revealing that the orders of the celestial beings are incalculable. Many are the blessed hosts of the extraterrestrial Intelligences, superior to our limited material numbers, and fully defined only by their thought, their extraterrestrial and celestial knowledge, happily donated by the divine Principle which is omniscient and the source of wisdom, equal to the superessential Principle, the creative Cause of being, Power and End that includes and embraces all beings.[8]

---

[6]See also, Isaiah 6:2, 3.
[7]Daniel 7:10; Revelation 5:11, 9:16.
[8]Dionysius the Areopagite, *The Celestial Hierarchies* (Godalmins, Surrey, UK: The Shrine of Wisdom, 1949), pp. 37–54.

Chapter 3

Lucifer
the Fallen Angel

How art thou fallen from heaven,
O Lucifer, son of the morning!
How art thou cut down to the ground,
which didst weaken the nations!
For thou hast said in thine heart,
"I will ascend into heaven,
I will exalt my throne
above the stars of God:
I will sit also upon the mount of the congregation,
in the sides of the north;
I will ascend above the heights of the clouds;
I will be like the most High."
Yet thou shalt be brought down to hell,
to the sides of the pit! (Isaiah 14:12–15)

In these lines, Isaiah summarizes the history of the rebellion of Lucifer "Son of the Morning" and his fall, which began the conflict between the angels who were faithful to God and those who took sides with the rebel. It is a myth that fascinated poets such as Dante and Byron.

According to Origen, there were also some "doubtful angels" who were uncertain whether to take the side of God or that of Lucifer. It was from these hesitant and irresolute creatures, who were permanently poised between good and evil and often unable to come to any definite decision, that humans are thought to have originated.

When did this division take place? It must have been before God introduced Adam and Eve to the Garden of Eden, since when they arrived the "tempter" was already there, alert and ready to act. On the other hand, though, after he had completed the creation and before he rested on the seventh day, God had seen that everything he had done "was good." This means that the rebellion had not yet taken place.

There is no detailed account in the bible of this rebellion against God, although it is briefly referred to in both the Old and New Testaments in particular, as we have seen, by Isaiah. In the Revelation of John the Divine it is stated that Lucifer took with him one third of the stars of heaven: "And there appeared another wonder in heaven; and behold a great red dragon, having seven heads and ten horns, and seven crowns upon his heads. An his tail drew the third part of the stars of heaven, and did cast them to the earth" (Revelation 12:3–4).

Another excerpt from the bible: "And it came to pass when men began to multiply on the face of the earth, and daughters were born unto them, that the sons of God saw the daughters of men and they were fair; and they took them wives of all which they chose" (Genesis 6:1–2) suggests another possible motive for the fall of the angels and their being led astray. And those angels that had lain on earth with the daughters of men became more and more evil. This angered God, who decided to exterminate them all, with the exception of Noah. This is the story of the flood. This second tradition which, as we have already seen, is reported also in the apocryphal Book of Enoch, although no mention is made of Lucifer. Thus a mystery remains as to his relationship with he who St. Paul refers to in his Epistle to the Ephesians (2:2) as the "prince of the power." But Ezekiel has this to say of him:

"Thou sealest up the sum, full of wisdom, and perfect in beauty. Thou hast been in Eden the garden of God; and every precious stone was thy covering, the sardius, topaz, and the diamond, the beryl, the onyx and the jasper, the sapphire, the emerald, and the carbuncle, and gold: the workmanship of thy tabrets and of thy pipes was prepared in thee in the day that thou wast created. Thou art the anointed cherub that covereth; and I have set thee so. . . . By the multitude of thy merchandise they have filled the midst of thee with violence, and thou hast sinned. . . . Thine heart was lifted up because of thy beauty, thou hast corrupted thy wisdom by reason of thy brightness . . . " (Ezekiel 28:12–17).

Lucifer "the bearer of light" was the most perfect, the most splendid of the angels that God had created to glorify him. But he was unable to continue to play this role and desired to rule the heavens in God's stead, to be the supreme authority. He committed the sin of pride and tried to appropriate unto himself that which did not belong to him.

Carefully considered, this is the same motive for the strife between fellow human beings. The conflict that was begun in heaven is continued on earth and involves us all, day in and day out. It is the power of good against that of evil, and it has happened since the beginning of time—still now as it was then, except that we have the promise that the powers of evil shall not prevail.

The existence of the Devil is an integral part of the doctrine of the Catholic Church. This has been reiterated by the various Popes, and not infrequently has been the subject of discussion among the faithful. In summing up this doctrine, Monsignor Corrado Balducci, who devoted many hours of profound study to the devil, has this to say in his book *La possessione diabolica*:

> Satan is first and foremost a creature of God, just like man, although with a nature and powers that are much superior. More precisely, he is a fallen angel.
>
> Even the angels, before they were able to enjoy eternal bliss, were put to the test. And a large number of them rebelled but were not granted—as humans have been—the possibility of redemption, because they were fully aware of their own condition and that of the divinity. From that moment there is talk of devils and hell.
>
> While the angels use their power to good purpose, the devils make use of theirs for maleficent and perverse ends, filled as they are with hatred for God and human beings. The Lord had it in his power to cast all the rebel angels into hell, thereby depriving them of any opportunity of doing harm. In his infinite wisdom and goodness, however, he allowed many of them to remain on this earth and exercise their maleficent powers although, in spite of themselves, they also represent an incentive toward

and a means of achieving moral perfection. In this sense, the devil can be said to be an instrument and perennial coefficient of sanctity. This design is most appropriate to the divine economy, which knows how to use everything, even the worst things of all, to do some good.[1]

This is a vast and extremely longsighted plan which turned a gesture of rebellion—that appears to have caused an irredeemable division into a potential good. The rebel angel thus, despite himself, became part of God's plan of redemption. He is an instrument for the perfecting of all humanity, and exposed as we are to temptation, we shall emerge victorious. This is the teaching of the Church.

The Fallen Angel According to Jakob Lorber

There is an extensive, poetic and gripping description— even if perhaps not a very orthodox one—of Lucifer's rebellion and fall in a singular text written by an unpretentious Austrian musician called Jakob Lorber. His story undoubtedly deserves to be told, and what he has to say to be repeated.

Jakob Lorber (1800–1864) was born and spent his life in Graz. On the morning of March 15, 1840, this simple man had an experience that deeply disturbed him. He heard a *voice* from an area "near his heart" which ordered him specifically to "take up his pen and write."[2]

---

[1]Corrado Balducci, *La possessione diabolica* (Rome: Edizioni Mediterranee, 1974). Translation from the Italian.

[2]Kurt Eggenstein, *The Prophet Jakob Lorber Predicts Coming Catastrophies and the True Christianity*, tr. Marjorie M. Schuck (St. Petersburg, FL: Valkyrie Publishing House, 1979), p. 5.

This event was to change his life completely for on that very day, he was due to send his acceptance to the theatre at Trieste, where he had been offered the post of second choirmaster—a most advantageous situation for him. However, when he had finished writing what the voice dictated to him that day, he realized that he was being entrusted with an exceptional task from on high that he would certainly be unable to fulfill if he took on the job at Trieste. He therefore refused the offer and also gave up the idea of getting married. He spent the rest of his life in almost complete retirement, living in a single room and scraping together a modest living by giving piano lessons.

Every day he spent hour after hour writing what the voice dictated. There are no corrections to his manuscript which, when printed after his death, filled over 10,000 pages.

Part of what Lorber wrote is of a scientific nature and contains descriptions of things and a knowledge that was quite unthinkable in his day. It appears that this information was given to him to show that it was the product of a mind that was divine and not human. Indeed, certain things he wrote about atoms, elementary particles, astrological information, and other subjects are seen to be exact and perfectly comprehensible today, although at that time no one was well enough informed to check the accuracy of what he wrote. It was, in fact, said that his writings were intended for the 20th-century world.

The other, and more extensive, part of what Lorber wrote is of a religious nature and is known as the New Revelation. Today a German publishing house is devoted to the circulation of his writings in German, and his works have been translated into many languages.[3] The New Revelation provides an explanation of the human being and the universe from our origins to the present day, and outlines a divine purpose that reveals the hidden meaning of the Scriptures. It is a monumental work and includes a description of the fall of Lucifer and his hosts.

For example, when the Divinity, by processes that will always remain mysterious, had identified and recognized in itself the creative spirit that comprehends everything, there arose a tension of great power. It then spake thus unto itself: "I will put my ideas outside myself, so that in them I may behold what my powers are able to achieve."[4]

He goes on to say that unless there is activity, the Divinity can know Itself only to a limited extent. Only through Its works can it learn more and more about Its own power and take delight in it, just the way every artist understands through his or her own creations what there is inside, and derives great joy from this. Thus, the Divinity wants to create and repeats to itself. "Within Me lies the power of the eternities; let us therefore create a being that shall be provided with all power like unto Myself, yet so that it bear within it the qualities through which I can recognize Myself."[5]

There was then created a spirit which was provided with all the powers, with the purpose of serenely dem-

---

[3]Kurt Eggenstein, *The Prophet Jakob Lorber Predicts Coming Catastrophies and the True Christianity*, p. 89. The voice dictated to Lorber in the first person. Lorber himself was convinced that it was the Lord himself who made him write what he did write.

[4]For information in English, contact the Valkyrie Publishing House, 8245 26th Ave. North, St. Petersburg, FL 33710, or write to the Lorber Society, Bietigheim 712, Wuerttemburg, Germany.

[5]Kurt Eggenstein, *The Prophet Jakob Lorber Predicts Coming Catastrophies and the True Christianity*, p. 88.

onstrating to the Divinity the powers that lay within it. This prime created spirit is called Lucifer (i.e., he who beareth the light), and people will understand why that should be his name. Lucifer bore within himself the light of awareness, and as the prime spiritual being was able to recognize clearly the limits of the interior spiritual polarity.

Lucifer—well aware that he had to represent in himself the opposite pole to God—believed that he was now in a position to absorb, in a certain sense, the Divinity into himself, and committed the error of believing he could assume into himself, as a created and therefore a finite being, even the infinite. . . . But the finite can never comprehend the infinite. Notwithstanding this, Lucifer, in his folly, believed he was able to make the Divinity his prisoner. In this way he lost his true position, distanced himself from the center of Divinity's heart, and was taken by the increasingly false desire to unite around himself as his own the creatures that had arisen from Divinity. Thus arose a conflict— i.e., a separation of the parts—which in the end caused Divinity to withdraw from Lucifer the power conferred on him, and Lucifer remained with his followers, but was deprived of power and creative strength.

The problem remained, of course, of what Divinity was to do with the host of the fallen: should Divinity annihilate Lucifer and all his followers, and then create a second Lucifer—who would probably have committed the same error, since to create a perfect spirit was inconceivable?

To achieve the enlightenment of self-awareness, the path followed was the only way. How could Lucifer, whose fall had taken place only because of an error, have subsequently gained the possibility of atoning for this error? Where would the wisdom of Divinity have been if it had not foreseen the possibility of a fall?

To better understand the complicated dynamics of the creation of the material universe as God willed it after Lucifer's rebellion, the Voice reported to Lorber that a crystal, once crystallized, can no longer be changed in its essence, and remains crystallized as a rhomboid, hexahedron, or an octahedron, depending on the form that corresponds to its nature. If the crystals are not perfectly pure, they must be dissolved by heat (love), and then crystallized again when the hot tide of love has cooled down, and this corresponds to the liberation of human will. At this point it is possible to form fine new crystals, and any prudent chemist is capable of producing crystals that are pure. And the Lord spoke again to Lorber:

> "You see, I am such a chemist! I dissolved the crystals that had become impure (Lucifer and his followers) in the warm waters of love, and then let these souls crystallize out again, that they might be crystal clear. You know that this happens in the ascent through the mineral and plant kingdoms to man. As the soul of Lucifer, however, encompasses the whole of physical creation, it must also find expression in the form of man."

> "For this, then, the material world, or the whole universe, or the man of material creation, was instituted. In him, the spirits were enveloped (clothed in matter according to the degree of their ill-will, exposed to struggles, temptations and suffering; in the first place, to get them

little by little to recognize their own faults, through the conditions having their influence on them and, secondly, in this way themselves to bring about their return, of their own free will. . . . Everywhere the principle of freedom is established as the first, and the principle of perfection as the second. . . . the whole of visible creation consists merely of particles of the great spirit Lucifer who has fallen and been bound to matter, and his followers."

"See what I am now doing on account of just one presumptuous angel! I tell you, never would earth nor sun, nor anything material have been created, if this one angel had remained free from pride. . . . In the growth of my innumerable not yet perfected children, in their increasing insight and perfection, and in their actions arising from this, lies also my most sublime joy. Their pleasure at greater perfection achieved with much effort is also my pleasure."[6]

It is impossible not to appreciate the grandeur and beauty of these words that—in my opinion—express an exceptional interpretation of Lucifer's rebellion against his Creator and the path chosen by God in His love to bring back *voluntarily* the rebel angel and the host of his followers into the celestial abode. Further on, on the question of the parable of the prodigal son, the Voice gave Lorber other explanations regarding Lucifer, the fallen angel. He said that in the scripture there is no chapter and verse that contains anything so great as the

---

[6]Kurt Eggenstein, *The Prophet Jakob Lorber Predicts Coming Catastrophies and the True Christianity* (St. Petersburg, FL: Valkyrie Publishing House, 1979), pp. 91, 93, 97, 98.

parable of the prodigal son. . . . In the name "Lucifer" is contained the whole substance of the son that is lost. Practically the whole of humanity today consists of nothing other than members of this "lost son," and precisely of those who are descended from the hapless seed of Adam. By "prodigal son" is meant every single individual. . . . and everyone who lives according to God's word is generated anew through the redemption, and the lost son (i.e., the essential nature) returns home.

To Lorber was also dictated the divine plan for bringing back the fallen spirits into the home of the Father along the material path. It will, however, take an inconceivably long time to achieve. There will come a time when no physical earth will rotate in infinite space, but a magnificent new spiritual creation of blessed and free spirits will everywhere fill infinite space and this most blessed condition shall never have an end. When this shall come to pass cannot be determined in terrestrial years, and even if we knew the number, we would be unable to comprehend it.[7]

On the basis of what was dictated to Lorber, material creation would be the means foreseen by the love of God to redeem and save the spirits that fell with Lucifer. The way of redemption that passes through the material is long and often painful, but in the end it brings us to God.

---

[7]Kurt Eggenstein, *The Prophet Jakob Lorber Predicts Coming Catastrophies and the True Christianity* (St. Petersburg, FL: Valkyrie Publishing House, 1979), p. 99.

Figure 3. St. Michael. Woodcut by A. Dürer, 15th century.

Chapter 4

Angels
and the Pope

Christian theology has always dealt with angels and tried to establish a genuine angelology. The Church Fathers and after them, the theologians, have discussed and contended over their nature in every possible way—what their duties are, whether they have bodies or are pure spirit, and much more besides.

There could not but have been a certain ambiguity: St. Paul did not look favorably on the cult of angels, but at the Council of Nicaea in A.D. 325, it was decreed that faith in angels was part of the dogma. But, shortly afterward in 343, at the Synod of Laodicea, the cult of angels was declared to be idolatrous. St. Augustine (354–430), however, claimed that *esse angelos novimus ex fide*, i.e., "that angels exist we know through faith." Finally, in 787, the Seventh Ecumenical Synod re-established a definite and limited cult of angels and archangels.

As is well known, and as I mentioned in the Foreword, not many people today bother about angels or believe they really exist. Even some theologians express a degree of doubt on the subject—but they have not been forgotten by the Popes. When he was still Patriarch of Venice, John Paul I claimed that "the angels are the great unknowns of our time." And he added: "It would, instead, be appropriate to remember them more often as ministers of Providence for the governance of mankind."

More recently, in the summer of 1986, John Paul II, too, spoke on several occasions about angels and repeated certain concepts "because they are discussed with ignorance." He made these statements during his general audiences on Wednesdays and they were duly reported in the press. The Pope has also dealt with the subject in an important publication.

He said that to doubt the existence of angels is "radically to revise Holy Scripture and with it the whole history of salvation." He defined the angels as "free and rational purely spiritual beings" and reiterated that "the truth about angels is inseparable from the central revelation, which is the existence, majesty and glory of God that shines over the whole visible and invisible creation."

The Pope reminded us that "the existence and works of angels is not the central part of the content of the divine word," and that "in his revelation, God is speaking above all to human beings." Nevertheless, although the angels "are not in the forefront of the reality of the revelation, they do altogether belong there, so much so that at certain moments we can see them performing fundamental tasks, in the name of God himself."

They are—says the Pope—intelligent and immortal, the voice, ears, and arms of God, present in an infinite number of religions. "By their nature, i.e., because of their spirituality, they are closer to God than any material creations, and almost constitute the environment closest to the Creator which is absolutely perfect spirit. It is for this reason that He is reflected above all in them. The bible provides a fairly explicit witness of this maximum nearness to God of the angels, of whom He speaks—in symbolical language—as His throne, His hosts and His heaven."

"The subject of angels," the Pope said on another occasion, "may seem extraneous or less vital to the mentality of modern people. Yet the Church, in frankly proposing the totality of the truth about God who also created the angels, believes it is doing human beings a great service. In this way the Church reminds us of the Christian revelation, according to which He is not only body, but also spirit. The Church confesses its faith in guardian angels, by venerating them in the liturgy of an apposite feast day (October 2nd) and recommends us to recall the protection (of our guardian angel) in frequent prayer."

The Pope's definition of the angels is as follows— "Creatures of a spiritual nature, gifted with intellect, and free will, superior to man."

He reminds us that Jesus said: "That in heaven . . . Angels *do always behold the face of my Father* which is in heaven" (Matthew 18:10). That "always behold the face of my Father" is the *highest manifestation of the adoration of God*. It may be said that it constitutes that *"celestial liturgy,"* performed in the name of the whole universe, with which is incessantly associated the terrestrial liturgy of the Church, especially in its culminating moments. It is sufficient to remember the act with which the Church, every day and at every hour, over the entire world, before beginning the Eucharistic Prayer, *at the heart of the Holy Mass,* recalls the Angels and Archangels in hymning the glory of God, thus uniting itself to those first of God's adorers.

The angels, the Pope says again, are also called upon to play their part in the story of salvation. We may read in the Epistle to the Hebrews (1:14): "Are they not all ministering spirits, sent forth to minister for them who shall be heirs of salvation?" Here, then, is sanctified by Holy Scripture the part played by guardian angels and protectors of humanity. On this, the Pope also quotes Psalms where it is written: "For he shall give his angels charge over thee to keep thee in all thy ways. They shall bear thee up in their hands lest thou dash thy foot against a stone" (Psalm 91:11).

And again: "[Jesus] also attributed to the angels the function of witnessing at the supreme divine judgment as to the fate of those who have recognized or denied Christ: 'Whosoever shall confess me before men, him shall the Son of man also confess *before the angels of God*: But he that denieth me before men shall be denied before the angels of God' (Luke 12:8–9). These words are significant because, if the angels are present at the last judgment, they must be concerned in the life of men."

The Pope has also spoken about the archangels Michael, Raphael, and Gabriel: "Lastly it is appropriate to notice that the Church honors with a liturgical cult three angels that are mentioned by name in Holy Scripture. The first is the *Archangel Michael*. The name sums up the essential attitude of the spirits of good. Mica-El, in fact, means 'Who like God?' This name expresses the choice leading to salvation by which the angels 'behold the face of the Father' that is in heaven. The second is *Gabriel* who is linked especially with the mystery of the incarnation of the Son of God. His name means 'In God is My strength,' or 'the strength of God,' almost as if to say that the culmination of the creation, the incarnation, is the supreme sign of the omnipotent Father. The third of these angels is called *Raphael*. Rafa-El means

'God healeth.' He made himself known in the story of Tobias in the Old Testament, which is significant in indicating how the little children of God are entrusted to the angels, because they are always in need of care, guardianship and protection."

On careful consideration, each of the three figures: Mica-El, Gabri-El and Rafa-El reflects in a particular manner the truth contained in the *question* raised by the author of the Epistle to the Hebrews (1:14): "Are they not all ministering spirits, sent forth to minister for them who shall be heirs of salvation?"

On the same occasion the Pope also spoke of "bad angels," explaining that the division of the angels into good and bad was not made at the moment of God's creation but on the basis of the free will of the creatures that were put to a test of a moral nature. When God created them as free beings, He was unable to provide against the possibility that they might sin.

The bad angels are pure spirits who deliberately chose to deny God. This was a radical and irreversible decision on a par with that of the good angels, but diametrically opposed to it: instead of accepting God in the fullness of His love, they made a denial that arose from a false sense of self-sufficiency, aversion and even hatred that developed into open rebellion.

"The *fall*," the Pope claims, "consists in the free choice of those spirits who were created, and who radically and irrevocably *denied God and His kingdom*, usurping His sovereign rights and attempting to subvert the economy of salvation and the very ordering of the entire creation. A reflection of this attitude is to be found in the words of the tempter to our progenitors: *ye shall be as gods* or *as God* (Genesis 3:5). Thus the evil spirit tried to plant in human beings the seed of rivalry, insubordination, and opposition to God, which became almost the motivation of His existence."

One might ask how it was that God did not pardon the sin of the angels. The Pope's answer is this: "Because they remain in their sin, *since they are eternally enchained by the choice that they made in the beginning* in denying God."

"The Devil," the Pope concluded, "is a blinded angel."

Chapter 5

The Angels
of Mystics and Saints

It is by no means rare to find encounters with angels in the lives of the mystics and saints. We shall now take a quick look at a few examples taken from the hagiography of past centuries, and then consider at greater length one or two recent and almost contemporary cases.

When Joan of Arc was 13, the archangel Michael appeared to her to announce that she was destined to save her country. He came in the guise of a shining and extremely handsome youth surrounded by angels, looking very warlike. Michael became Joan's guide, and performed a number of tasks for her—finding her lost sword, advising her as to what flag to lead her troops under, and constantly encouraging her to carry out her duty. At her trial, which ended so tragically, when she was interrogated at great length and in detail by her judges, she told them she had seen angels on numerous occasions. She also said that the archangel Michael touched the ground as he walked. But to her judges this sounded unreal and probably false. Even after she was condemned to the stake, she did not retract a word of what she had said.

The blessed Angela of Foligno (1248–1309) declared that she had been filled with great joy at the sight of angels. She said that if she had not experienced it, she would not have believed that the sight of angels could bring such joy. Angela, a wife and mother, was converted in 1285 after living a life that the hagiographers wrote off as "dissolute." She made a full confession and took the mystic path that was to make her a perfect bride of Christ, who appeared to her in visions accompanied by angels on several occasions.

Agnese of Montepulciano, another mediaeval mystic, received—according to the chroniclers—communion from an angel as many as ten times, thus avoiding having to interrupt her conversation with God. More than once she was consoled by a vision of angels, one of whom ordered her to build a monastery.

Saint Rosa of Viterbo (1235–1252), who declared her intention of going into a convent at age 7, lived a short but intense life, full of miraculous events and healings. An angel appeared to her often, predicting future events including the death of the Emperor Frederick II.

Saint Claire of Montefalco (1268–1308) was known as Sister Claire of the Cross because of her great devotion to the crucified Jesus. A very beautiful girl from a well-to-do family, she dedicated her life to God, and at the age of 6 was allowed to enter the house of prayer founded by her elder sister Joan. Extraordinary events occurred throughout her life, especially visions, apparitions, and victorious struggles with the devil. Angels appeared to her several times in the course of visions of the nativity, crucifixion, and resurrection of Jesus. Forbidden to receive communion with the other sisters, she received it—it is written in the chronicles—in her own cell, from Jesus himself, who was accompanied by many angels.

Joan—Claire's sister—was visited by angels since she had rendered herself worthy by her innocence and the perfect purity of her life for an angel of the Lord to visit her almost every night. During the last years of her life this angel came down to her while she was praying and allowed her to hear the music of paradise. And Claire also enjoyed the same privilege. On a number of occasions their sister nuns all heard the celestial music and saw the room become filled with a splendid light as the angel descended.

Claire was extremely humble throughout her life, ate nothing but bitter grasses and hard bread, slept on bare boards, and went barefoot even in winter. She was continually immersed in contemplation of the passion and death of Jesus, and ardently longed to become one with him. This boundless love of hers for the crucified Christ is connected with the most exceptional event of her life. Jesus once appeared to her in the form of an extremely handsome youth, dressed as a pilgrim and with a heavy cross round his neck, which rendered him extremely fatigued and weary. Claire asked in the name of grace to be allowed to bear that cross herself and, in answer, was told that it would be planted without delay right in the middle of her heart. From that moment, the holy Virgin had not the slightest doubt that she bore within herself the real and true effigy of her crucified Lord.[1]

Indeed, since Claire had confided this to some of her sisters, after her death it was decided to find out if what she had said was true. Her body was opened up

---

[1]This story was told by Padre Luca di San Giuseppe in *Santa Chiara di Monte Falco* (Trevi: Tipografia Nazzarena, 1889).

and her heart found to be larger than the head of a young child. When it was opened, inside were found impressed in relief, in flesh, the symbols of the passion—a cross with the figure of Jesus on it, a scourge, the crown of thorns, the nails, the reed and the sponge. This miraculous event was confirmed by a number of reliable witnesses, including laymen.

Seventy years earlier, St. Francis had received the stigmata visibly on his hands, feet, and ribs; Claire received them invisibly impressed directly on her heart. When Claire died at age 40, another prodigy took place: "Everyone present, both nuns and priests," we can read in the same volume by Padre Luca, "saw descend from on high a clarity of marvelous splendor, which alighted first on Claire's brow, surrounded her and then covered the whole of her face"; and while they were all observing this miracle full of amazement, Claire's soul flew up into heaven—certainly accompanied by those angels that had throughout her life appeared to her in the form of "winged youths."

The case of Santa Francesca Romana (1384–1440), the saint best known to and loved by the Romans, also deserves special mention. She was a beautiful and intelligent girl born to a rich family. She wanted to become a bride of Christ, but in obedience to her father agreed to marry a Roman patrician, becoming an exemplary wife and mother. Throughout her life she managed to reconcile the cares of family life with the strain of her spiritual and mystical leanings until, having been left a widow, she was free to dedicate herself totally to her religious vocation. Santa Francesca founded the Order of Oblates of Mary, who still live in the monastery of Tor de'Specchi, close to the Theatre of Marcello in Rome.

This saint was in the company of angels for most of her life, and of one angel in particular who she saw and heard close beside her. The first appearance of this angel was in 1399 when he acted as a "bathing attendant" and saved the lives of Francesca and her sister-in-law, Vannuzza, when they fell into the Tiber. He appeared as a boy of 10, with long hair and brightly shining eyes, dressed in a white tunic, like those worn by subdeacons during liturgies. He performed the task of guardian and guide, but also served as a chastiser when the occasion arose. He was often at Francesca's side during the numerous and violent struggles she had with the devil.

This youthful angel remained at the saint's side for twenty-four years, and then another took his place who was very much more resplendent than the first, of a superior hierarchy, and who remained with her until her death. He often appeared in the act of spinning and weaving a golden thread—that of the saint's life. When she was about to die, Francesca saw the angel spinning faster and faster as the thread of her life drew to its close.

The 15th-century frescoes by Antoniazzo Romano in the chapel of her monastery represent several occasions on which she was accompanied by angels, bearing witness to this supernatural presence beside her. Francesca was very much loved by the people of Rome for her exceptional charity and the miraculous healings she performed.

●   ●   ●

Francis of Assisi, the quintessence of Italian sainthood, received the stigmata in 1224 on Mount Verna, to which he used to retreat in prayer and meditation, and where he often turned his thoughts to the archangel Michael. One morning, while he was absorbed in contemplation of the sacrifice of Christ, in the silence and solitude of his mountain top, he saw coming toward him a seraph with six fiery wings and the face of a crucified man. While he contemplated this most beautiful image, he felt that something great and mysterious was happening to him and was suddenly aware that wounds had opened in his hands and feet that appeared to have been caused by coarse nails, and his chest also began to bleed.

This is what happened in the time-honored description by San Bonaventura of Bagnoregio (1217-1257), who as almost a contemporary of St. Francis is better equipped than anyone else to provide documentary detail of the story: "One morning, at about the season of the feast of the Exaltation of the Cross, while praying alone on a mountain top (Francis) saw a Seraph with six fiery and brightly shining wings descend from heaven. If flew very swiftly close to the place where the man of God was, and the image of a crucified man appeared between its wings, with hands and feet arranged in the form of a cross, as if nailed to one. Two of the wings sprung from the head, two were open in flight and two covered the whole body.

"At the sight, the Saint was astonished and his heart was filled with mixed feelings of sadness and joy. He was, in fact, delighted at the gracious look he was granted from the face of the Christ below the image of the Seraph; but, when he saw that he was crucified, his soul felt as if pierced by a swordstroke of grevious compassion.

"He was utterly amazed by this vision which he failed to understand, well knowing that the pain of the passion can in no way be reconciled with the beatitude of a Seraph. In the end, however, the Lord made him understand that this vision had been granted to his eyes by divine Providence, so that he, a friend of Jesus Christ, should be forewarned that he was to become totally transformed to resemble the crucified Christ, not with the martyrdom of his flesh but by the kindling of a flame of love in his spirit.

"When the vision faded, a wonderful ardor remained in the heart of Francis. And even in his flesh there remained the impression of the no less wonderful symbols of the passion of Christ. Immediately there began to appear in his hands and feet the marks of the nails, just as he had a short while before seen in the image of the crucified man. His hands and feet were as if the nails had pierced through them. The heads of the nails could be seen on the palms of his hands and the upper part of his feet, while the points protruded from the opposite side. Furthermore, the heads of the nails, both on his hands and feet, were rounded and black, and the points were long, and bent back as if hammered so that, once they had passed through the flesh, they remained totally above it. His right side, too, was as if it had been pierced by a spear, tinged red by a wound from which blood issued frequently, staining his tunic and undergarment. . . . "[2]

Only after a great deal of hesitation did the Saint decide to tell his brethren what had happened to him and give them full details of what he had seen in his vision. San Bonaventura adds, however, "He who had appeared to him had said certain things that he would never be able to reveal to anyone in his lifetime. It is therefore to be believed that the words of that Seraph, who had appeared miraculously in the form of a cross, are so full of mystery that it is not permitted to utter

---

[2]From San Bonaventura da Bagnoregio, *Vita di San Francesci d'Assisi* (Rome: Edizioni Porziuncola, 1985). Translated from the Italian.

them to men." Francis did, indeed, tell his brethren that, "My secret is for me alone."

Angels played an important role in the life of Saint Francis. The ancient church called the Portiuncula, dedicated to the Mother of God and situated near Assisi had, for example, been known from the earliest times as Santa Maria degli Angeli. Celestial spirits, San Bonaventura tells us, often visited the place. So, because of his great devotion to the angels and the Mother of Christ, Saint Francis decided to restore the church and reside beside it with his brethren.

Once, when he was so weak that he was unable to move, Francis was consoled by the music of angels: "When he was so weak because of his infirmity," we read again in San Bonaventura, "he felt a desire to hear the sound of an instrument to raise his spirits. And, lo, a band of angels appeared to satisfy his desire. . . . " Their music provided the Saint with such delight that he imagined he was already in another world and his most intimate brethren also heard it.

The devotion of Saint Francis to angels is described by San Bonaventura in these words: "He was united by an inseparable bond of love to the angels, those spirits that burn with a marvelous fire and, with this, penetrate into God and inflame the souls of the chosen. In sign of his devotion to them, beginning on the feast of the Assumption of the Most Holy Virgin, he fasted for forty days, praying continually. His great zeal for the salvation of the souls of everyone made him particularly devoted to the Archangel Michael, whose duty it was to present souls to God."

Saint Francis was the first Roman Catholic to receive the stigmata. That the wounds of Christ appeared prodigiously in him is testified by witnesses above suspicion, and it was this that put the seal on his vocation to complete Jesus's work of redemption.

• • •

Centuries later, much closer to our own time, Padre Pio da Pietralcina received the stigmata in a similar manner. Francesco Forgione—this was Padre Pio's real name—felt a vocation for the priesthood at a very early age. He was only 5 years old when, in 1892, he experienced for the first time charismatic favors, ecstasy, and saw apparitions. Both the Madonna and the Sacred Heart of Jesus appeared to him. At the same age, however, there also began his "diabolical apparitions" which, as he himself wrote in his diary: "were always in most obscene form, human but above all bestial." These were the first attacks by the Evil One, who was to torment Padre Pio throughout his life. But he also had a vision that gave him strength and always sustained him: he saw beside him a majestic figure of a man of rare beauty, as resplendent as the sun who took him by the hand and encouraged him, inviting him specifically to: "Come with me because it is meet that you should fight like a valiant warrior."[3]

During the numerous and extremely hard-fought battles, Padre Pio was obliged to sustain with the Evil One, a luminous figure (an angel?) was always at his side, helping him and giving him strength. On its first appearance it had also assured him of final victory.

Francesco Forgione (our Padre Pio) donned the habit of a Capuchin friar in 1903 and was ordained priest seven years later. Until 1916, because of his pre-

---

[3]Fernando da Riese, *Padre Pio da Pietralcina* (Ed. P. Pio da Pietralcina, 1984).

carious health, he remained at home, but was then sent to San Giovanni Rotondo, where he could benefit from the clear mountain air, for what was intended to be a provisional stay, but lasted for the remaining fifty-two years of his life.

The young friar soon earned a reputation for himself. Even before he received the stigmata, people recognized him as having been sent by God, and began to besiege him. He was obliged to spend as long as nineteen hours in succession in the confessional and was constantly assailed by a "throng of souls athirst for God."

On the night between the 5th and 6th of August 1918, Padre Pio was granted the mysterious divine recompense: while he was hearing the confessions of some boys on the evening of the 5th, a celestial personage appeared to him with "a kind of tool that looked like a very long, well-sharpened steel blade that seemed to have been forged in fire" in his hand. The celestial personage struck Padre Pio "in the soul" with this tool. Padre Pio moaned, and an endless spasm overcame him. This was the first stigma, that in his side.

On September 20th of the same year, after mass, the work was completed, again by an angelical figure. Here is the description of what happened in Padre Pio's own words: "I saw before me a mysterious figure, similar to the personage I had seen on August 5th, with the only difference that blood was dripping from its hands, feet and side. I was frightened by the sight: I shall never be able to tell you what I felt at that moment. I felt I was dying and should have died if the Lord had not intervened to stay my heart which I felt to be leaping out of my breast. The vision of the personage faded, and I saw that my hands, feet and side had been pierced and blood was trickling from them. . . . Just imagine the torment I felt then, and continue to feel almost every day."[4]

•   •   •

The other great mystic of our day, Teresa Neumann, Padre Pio's contemporary, was in serene daily contact with the angels. Before we speak of this, certain things need to be said about Teresa, who was born in the village of Konnersreuth in Bavaria in 1898 and died there in 1962.

She was born into a poor and devotedly religious family, but one free from any taint of bigotry. She would have liked to become a missionary nun, but a serious illness—the result of an accident that left her blind and paralyzed—prevented her from doing so. She was confined to bed for many years, serenely bearing her infirmity, only to be unexpectedly cured first of her blindness and then her paralysis through the intervention of Saint Teresa of Lisieux, to whom she was devoted, and who appeared to her several times announcing that she would soon be cured and revealing the exceptional destiny that was in store for her. And not long afterward she began to have the visions of the passion of Christ that were to come to her, every Friday, for the rest of her life. The stigmata also began gradually to appear in her. Subsequently, Teresa felt less and less need of nourishment and, after a short time, completely stopped eating and drinking. That she continued to fast totally for as long as thirty-six years was established without a shadow of doubt by commis-

---

[4]Fernando da Riese, *Padre Pio da Pietralcina* (Ed. P. Pio da Pietralcina, 1984).

sions set up by the Bishop of Ratisbon, in whose diocese Konnersreuth lies.

The stigmata, fasting, and visions were the constant features of Teresa's life. The stigmata were always painful and bled during her visions on Fridays. Her fasting is a clear symbol of the power of the eucharist. She, herself, said that she was kept alive "by the Savior," i.e., the consecrated host she received every day and, as was proved, remained intact in her until the moment of her next communion.

Teresa had visions almost every day of her life. They involved a sudden rapture that removed her completely from the time and place in which she was, so that she became invisible to every earthly thing. Her visions were of the passion and death of Jesus and other events of his life, and of those of the Madonna, saints, and apostles. During these visions she spoke in Aramaic and other languages that under normal circumstances she did not know (as a simple peasant girl she spoke only her local dialect, as experts and university teachers were able to ascertain). Between visions she was in what was termed a "state of tranquillity" in which she described to those present what she had seen, and answered their questions.

More than once Teresa Neumann's visions were of the world of angels—those mentioned in the Bible and her own guardian angel. She perceived the presence of her guardian angel as the "luminous figure" of a man on her right-hand side. She also saw the angels of people who came to visit her. She maintained that her angel protected her from the devil, took her place in moments of bilocation (she was often seen in two places at the same time) and helped her in moments of difficulty.

She also had the gift of being able to assist people at the moment of death and attend the judgment that took place immediately after they had died. We have the direct witness of her friend Anni Spiegl, who was present on both occasions, of what happened at the death of her sister Ottilia, a woman who had lived a saintly life, and of her father Ferdinand:

"At the very moment when Ottilia died, Teresa had a vision: her face was so serene and transfigured that I understood she was present at the occurrence of a great event. Finally, she looked aloft and said: 'With you, with you!' and it seemed as if she wanted to raise herself. Later on, Teresa told me that her dead mother, her brother Engelbert who died when 45 years old, and her younger brother who died at age 2 had come to receive her. Teresa then saw the Savior, who arrived suddenly and looked tenderly at Ottilia. All then disappeared together into a bright light, and she would have liked to follow them."[5]

When, in the same year (1958), her father died, Teresa again saw the same dead relatives return with Ottilia to receive their aged father, together with his guardian angel. This time, though, the Savior did not take Ferdinand her father with him immediately. He remained behind with his guardian angel looking sadly after the group as it moved away. A few months later, Teresa was able to say that her father was in paradise. His period of purgatory had evidently been extremely short.

On many other occasions Teresa Neumann had visions of angels and archangels busy performing the

---

[5]Anni Spiegl, *Leben und Sterben der Therese Neumann von Konnersreuth* (Kloster Theresianum, 1976) and Johannes Steiner, *Visionen der Therese Neumann* (Verlag Schell & Steiner, 1979). Subsequent material explaining St. Teresa is quoted from the same sources.

tasks and missions that are ascribed to them in the Gospel. This, for example, is the vision of the annunciation, as reported by Dr. Johannes Steiner, who was present and heard Teresa's description.

"Teresa saw a young woman, still almost a girl, deep in prayer in a small house. Suddenly, there appeared before her a luminous man (a term Teresa used to describe the angels). He had not entered but was simply there. I asked Teresa at this point: 'Did he have wings?' And she replied: 'Whatever do you mean? The luminous men do not need wings!'

"The luminous man bent over the frightened girl and said: *Schelam lich, Mirjam, gaseta.* . . . Mary, still frightened but with a more trusting expression, looked at the luminous figure. The angel spoke other weighty words. She asked the angel something, and the angel replied. When the angel had finished speaking, the girl bowed her head and said a word or two. At that very moment Teresa saw a great light from on high enter into the girl, as the angel bowed and disappeared."

The bringing of glad tidings to the shepherds was seen by Teresa in this way: "Half an hour after midnight, after Teresa had witnessed the birth of the Redeemer, she saw herself transported to a hut on the top of a low hill, about twenty minutes distant from the stable. There, eight shepherds were used to shelter at night. Suddenly, it became light and everyone in the hut was afraid. Warily, they peered out and there, in a cloud of light at a height of about three meters, they saw an angel, as the figure of a young man fashioned of light, in a splendid white robe with long sleeves and a belt. It was the same angel that had spoken to Mary (i.e., the archangel Gabriel). His left hand was placed on his chest and his right was raised. He had no wings. All the surrounding countryside was filled with a bright light that emanated from him. The angel then addressed the shepherds to reassure them in a clear, friendly and solemn voice, speaking their own language. He twice pointed toward the left with his right hand. When he had finished speaking, a multitude of angels appeared around him, they too luminous and on shining clouds. Together they sang a marvelous song which the shepherds listened to, paying close attention. The band of angels then disappeared. The shepherds discussed among themselves before moving off in the direction of Bethlehem."

• • •

We leave Teresa Neumann at this point to meet a great Italian mystic, *Teresa Palminota*, who died in Rome in 1934 at the age of only 38. She had all her life been the protagonist of exceptional events. She had extrasensory perceptions, bore the stigmata, fasted for over three years, experienced unbelievable thermic phenomena in that a mysterious fire emanated from her breast and literally burned anyone who came into contact with her.

Teresa's life was solitary and reserved. She never disclosed the secret of her stigmata and other extraordinary events to anyone except her confessor and spiritual guide, Father Luigi Fizzotti. He knew what had happened in her soul and left a witness of it in his book *Il segreto di Teresa* which was published posthumously.[6]

She, too, was on familiar terms with her guardian angel, who she used to call "my little angel," and to whom she attributed many spiritual happenings and actual appearances. As the result of prurient otitis,

---

[6]Luigi Fizzotti, *Il seqreto di Teresa* (Ed. Eco, S. Gabriele, 1980).

Teresa had become stone deaf. This fact has been confirmed by her doctors and all who came into contact
with her. When, however, she was with her spiritual
guide she heard quite clearly everything he had to say,
even without looking him in the face. It can therefore be
excluded that she was lip reading him. When Father
Fizzotti asked her for an explanation, she replied that it
was either the Lord, or else her "little angel" who
enabled her to understand everything.

This little angel helped her on many occasions:
when Father Fizzotti visited her, Teresa always opened
the door just as he was putting his hand to the bell. She
said that this was the work of her angel, who informed
her that the Father was about to arrive. When she went
to visit her Confessor, although she was not in the habit
of warning him in advance, she never arrived and
found him out. When questioned about this, she said
that before leaving home she asked Jesus or her little
angel if she was to go or not—always getting the right
answer. On one occasion it even happened that Father
Fizzotti warned her not to come to see him as he would
not be in. But Teresa went all the same and found him
at home because something unexpected had kept him
there! On this occasion, too, it was her little angel who
informed her.

Teresa also received angelic assistance on specific
occasions, such as the time when she was living with
her family, and she tried to type a text for her sister
though she had never put a finger to a typewriter. Her
fingers were numb from the pain of the stigmata, and
all attempts were in vain, until she asked her little angel
to help. Shortly afterward Teresa's sister received her
text, complete and faultlessly typed.

The life of Teresa Palminota was filled with pleasant happenings. When she was out walking, she was followed step-by-step by a butterfly that stopped to play with her every time she sat down to rest. She was convinced, and told her Confessor, that the butterfly was her angel, and added that she had sometimes seen it change into a little angel.

Teresa Palminota, Teresa Neumann and Padre Pio are all in process of being declared blessed.

Natuzza Evolo's Angels

Natuzza Evolo, of Paravati in Calabria, is an extraordinary figure of our time. Married and the mother of numerous children, she is now over 60 and apparently an ordinary Southern Italian woman. Exceptional events have, however, always happened to her. She is able to heal people who are desperately ill, and has the gifts of telepathy and clairvoyance. Words written in blood appear on her body and, during Easter week, the stigmata open on her hands, feet, and side.

She also speaks to the dead and meets her guardian angel. What is more, she claims that she can constantly see people's guardian angels close to them. Natuzza is a very humane person, able to help anyone in need, but extremely humble and reserved in everything that concerns herself. Professor Luigi Lombardi Satriani, an anthropologist, and Dr. Mariela Boggio nevertheless succeeded in making a documentary film about her which was shown in Italy in 1985. This is what Natuzza had to say about her angel and other phenomena, in answer to the questions of her interviewers.

"Natuzza, for many years thousands of people have come to you, and you have something to say to them all, give to them all. Why do they come? What needs do they tell you about? What do they ask you to do for them?"

"They ask about their illnesses, whether their doctors have prescribed the right cure, things of that sort. . . . Then they ask about those who have died, whether they are in heaven or purgatory, if they are in need."

"And how do you manage to reply to them? What do you say, for example, when they ask you about the dead?"

"I can recognize the dead if I met them up to, say, two or three months before; if not, I recognize them from their photographs."

"So, when they show you their photographs, you are even able to tell them where they are now?"

"If they are in paradise, or in purgatory, and if they are in need, if they have a message to send to their relatives."

"And can you also give the dead messages from their living, relations?"

"Yes, yes, and the living, too."

"You say you can see an angel close to people . . . "

"Yes, yes, close to them. Not to everyone, but nearly everyone."

"Is it only the living who have angels?"

"Only the living, not the dead."

"And where is this angel with respect to the person?"

"With respect to the person, on the right. On the left of priests. Sometimes it happens that a priest comes in plain clothes, but I understand he is a priest because I see the angel on the left. When I kiss his hand he asks me 'How did you know?' and I tell him 'I can see your angel on the left' . . . "

Monte Sant'Angelo

San Michele al Gargano is a place with an intense atmosphere, very well known in Italy and abroad. It is an ancient little town, perched on a hill in this Apulean promontory, looking down on the sea. It is famous for the cult of the Archangel Michael and his apparitions there. His first appearances are legendary, dating back to the fifth century A.D. It is said that in 490, when paganism still thrived on Mount Gargano, a bull was seen on its knees in front of an inaccessible cave. The Bishop of Siponto, San Lorenzo Maiorano, ordered three days of prayer and fasting. At the end of them, the Archangel Michael appeared and said: "I am the Archangel Michael and live always in God's presence. This cave is sacred to me, I chose it. I myself am its vigilant guardian. . . . There, where the rock opens, people's sins can be forgiven. Whatever is asked for in prayer here will be granted. Go, therefore, up onto the mountain and dedicate the cave to Christianity."

But the Bishop put off carrying out the angel's orders because of the difficulty of doing so. Two years later, Christian Siponto was besieged by the pagans of Odoacre. When all seemed lost, the Bishop obtained a truce for three days and devoted them to prayer. Surely enough, the Archangel appeared again and promised to help Siponto win the forthcoming battle. And, indeed, a storm of sand and hail blew up and put the pagan hordes to flight. Bishop Lorenzo staged a procession up the Archangel's mountain, but did not have the courage to go into the cave.

In 493, on the anniversary of his first appearance, the Archangel came again to the Bishop and ordered him to enter the cave. He also told him that he had himself consecrated the place, and thus there was no need for anyone else to do so. In the end the Bishop obeyed and went into the cave where he found an altar the archangel had prepared, with a red cloth over it on which a cross of crystal had been placed. This cave, the only place of worship that was never consecrated by a human being, has been known through the centuries as the Celestial Basilica.

It is also related that the Emperor Henry II, known as the Saint (973–1024), went on a pilgrimage to Mount Gargano two years before he died, and had himself shut inside the cave alone for a whole night. There, he had a vision of a band of brightly shining angels, led by the Archangel Michael, and witnessed a celestial liturgy. This extraordinary experience took on mystical value for the king and served as his initiation.

The Archangel's last appearance was in 1656, when Gargano was stricken by the plague and thousands died. Archbishop Alfonso Piccinelli invoked the Archangel Michael, who appeared on September 25th and told him: "I am the Archangel Michael. Anyone who takes a stone from this cave will be cured of the plague. Bless the stones and engrave on one of them a cross and my name." And it was so—the people took up stones in faith and the plague died out.

The sacred cave, which has been a place of pilgrimage for centuries, is now a grandiose spectacle, adorned with splendid works of art. In the middle, preserved in an urn of silver and Bohemian crystal, is a magnificent marble statue by Sansovino of the Archangel Michael, represented in the attitude of a victorious warrior trampling underfoot a repugnant monster.

The 24 panels of the great bronze doors for the Basilica were forged in Constantinople in 1076. The panels are a work of art of inestimable value, and are dedicated to angelic appearances related in the Old and New Testaments.

Loreto

Is this Sanctuary a relic from the Holy Land? "The faithful believe so and will have no truck with any doubt about it. Was it built from materials left on the Adriatic coast by pilgrims from Palestine? This stimulating idea is worthy of respect and calm consideration. I allow myself to draw your attention to it since, as a citizen of the Lagoon of Venice, there come to my mind the countless religious treasures and works of art that reached Venice by sea from the East. If anyone considers this theory to be sacrilegious, let him know that I am not imposing it; if anyone else is of the opinion that it is baseless, let him say so." These fine words of Monsignor Loris Capovilla, the Papal delegate to the Sanctuary of Loreto, serve as the best possible introduction to the ancient and stimulating enigma of the translocation of the Holy House, which, according to tradition, was flown by angels from Palestine to Loreto.

The "Loreto question" is complex and it would take a lot of space to deal adequately with it. We must necessarily be content here with a brief summary, and refer those interested to the specialist literature on the subject.

The Holy House, venerated at Loreto and preserved inside the Basilica, is held to be the one in which the Virgin Mary was born and the Annunciation took place. Many ancient texts confirm that the House was venerated in Palestine for centuries.

In 1291, Crusaders in the Holy Land guarding sacred places were violently attacked by the Turks and had to abandon the country. Historians maintain that the translocation of the Holy House from Nazareth to the West was closely linked with the enforced and definitive retreat of the Crusaders from Palestine.

The well-documented Loreto tradition also has it that the House of the Virgin Mary—which was removed from Nazareth in 1291—was first deposited on a hill on the coast of Illyria, near a river. "The angels of God," reads an authoritative text preserved at Teramo, "brought the said church with them and placed it in a certain castle called River."

Subsequently, in 1294, the House was again transported from Illyria, to Italy, to the province of Ancona, where it was located in a number of places before being finally established at Loreto.

Father Giuseppe Santarelli, who has devoted long years of learned study to the Loreto question, observes that the translocation of the Holy House fits perfectly into the historical climate of the period of the Crusades: "Everyone knows, indeed"—we can read in his carefully documented book on the Holy House of Loreto— "that the 'famous' relics from the Crusades, which were brought to the West, are remarkable examples of devotion and art," one example of which, that of the Holy Shroud, will serve for them all. "Famous," too, however, became all manner of things that had to do with the lives of Jesus, the Virgin Mary and the apostles— their clothes, sacred objects, earth, and stones. The celebrated *Camposanto* at Pisa originated from precisely this custom. Archbishop Ubaldo de'Lanfranchi, on a pilgrimage to the Holy Sepulchre, caused earth from that holy place to be dug up, loaded into Pisan ships and spread around the Major Church in 1203, at the place where the Cathedral and Baptistery ("leaning tower") were later to be constructed.

The Crusaders brought from the Middle East works of art, statues, columns, and the remains of ancient monuments. Considered in this historical perspective, and remembering that many of the inhabitants of the Marches went on the Crusades, it seems reasonable that the Holy House may have been translocated in this manner.

The Holy House itself is built of ancient, smoke-blackened bricks and stones, and preserves the remains of paintings and graffiti. There are no foundations, and it appears that not long after it was moved, pilgrims to the Holy Land checked that the perimeter of the House at Loreto was exactly that of the foundations which had remained at Nazareth. Archeological research has also proved that the House originated from the Middle East at the time of the Crusades.

As regards the ancient and devoutly believed tradition that it was angels who actually transported it, two alternative theories can be considered. There is the tradition of the "angel-monks." Early authors, and especially the Eastern ones, often used to compare the life of monks with that of the angels, and claimed that those monks who led angelic lives ended up by looking like angels. At the time of the Crusades, there were in Palestine military orders, including the Templars, who took a triple vow to defend pilgrims, the holy places, and relics. It is therefore reasonable to suppose that the "angel-monks" responsible for the translocation to the West—by sea—of the Holy House were, in fact, the Templars.

The other theory that is worth a thought is that the translocation was made by members of the house of a Byzantine family called Angeli and, in the imagination and devotion of the people, as time passed they became identified with the angels of heaven.

Santarelli rightly claims that "the fundamental thing about the Holy House is the *message*, and the *miracle* of its translocation. All the same, the stimulating tradition that the House, in which the Annunciation, the greatest event in the history of Christianity took place, was borne on the wings of angels has persisted through the centuries and is deeply rooted in the minds of the people. It has not lost its fascination even in this materialist and rationalistic age.[7]

It therefore seemed both right and proper that the matter should be discussed in a book on guardian angels.

The Angels of Fatima and Garabandal

The apparitions of the Madonna at Fatima are too well known for us to need to say a great deal about them here. They took place in 1917 to three shepherd children: Lucia, who was 10 years old, her cousin Francisco who was 9, and Jacinta, Francisco's sister, who was only 7. All three were good, simple, strong, healthy, and rather timid. None of them could read or write. They used to take their sheep to pasture together and spend long hours there, playing among the flowers in the fields. They were pious and devoted, as their families were bringing them up to be. Their mothers taught them the catechism in the evenings, and they said the rosary together every day.

Before the Madonna appeared to them, an angel did, an angel who seemed to have been given the duty of preparing them for what was about to happen. The first time was in 1915, and only Lucia of the three was a witness. She was then 8 years old and with other little

---

[7]Giuseppe Santarelli, *La Santa Casa di Loreto* (Loreto, 1988).

girls on a hill near Aljustrel. They all suddenly saw a strange snow-white figure arise among the trees. It was midday and the sun's rays made the figure almost transparent. The girls were amazed and rather afraid. Instinctively they began to say a prayer together, keeping their eyes fixed on the shining figure. By the time they had finished the prayer the figure had disappeared.

A year went by and, in the Spring of 1916, on a drizzly day, Lucia and her little cousins were taking shelter in a small cave from which they could still watch their sheep. After they had eaten their lunch and prayed, they began to play, and, as they did so, a strong gust of wind made them look up and see—above the trees in front of the cave—a white figure which, this time, did not remain still. It advanced toward them, as if blown on the wind. As it got closer, they were able to make out more clearly its face and features, which were those of a youth of superhuman beauty who must have been about 15 years old.

This is how Lucia later described this meeting: "It came up to us and said: 'Don't be afraid! I am the angel of peace. Pray with me!' and, kneeling down, bent its head to the ground. A supernatural feeling made us do the same and repeat the words we heard it say: 'My God! I believe, adore profoundly, hope and Love Thee! I ask Thy pardon for those who neither believe, nor adore, nor hope and do not love Thee.' The figure repeated this three times then stood up and said: 'Pray with these words. The hearts of Jesus and Mary will listen to the voice of your supplications.' And it disappeared. The supernatural atmosphere that surrounded them was so intense that we were hardly aware of our existence. For a long time we remained in the position in which it had left us, repeating the same oration over

and over. The presence of God was so intense and intimate that we dared not speak even among ourselves.
The next day our spirits were still enveloped in that
atmosphere which began to fade only very slowly."[8]

A few months later, between July and August,
while the children were playing in the orchard of
Lucia's home, the same person appeared again and
invited them to pray, constantly offer orations and
make sacrifices to the Lord. The angel added that it was
the guardian angel of Portugal, the angel of peace:
"Accept and humbly bear the suffering that the Lord
will send you." It was a real and proper investiture that
gradually brought the children to awareness that something extraordinary was about to happen and it was up
to them to be worthy.

Another few months passed and, when the children were in the cave where the angel appeared to
them and they had recited together the prayer it had
taught them, it appeared again. It was more splendid
than ever, looked just like snow, and held a chalice in
its hand on which there was a host, from which drops
of blood fell into the chalice.

The angel then knelt down beside the children,
leaving the brightly-shining chalice and host miraculously suspended in air. It invited them to repeat three
times this prayer: "Most Holy Trinity, Father, Son and
Holy Spirit, I adore Thee and offer Thee the most precious body, blood, soul and divinity of Jesus Christ who
is present in all the tabernacles on earth, to make
amends for the outrage, sacrilege and indifference
which are an offense unto Himself. And through the
infinite merit of his Most Holy Heart and the Immacu-

---

[8]Icilio Felici, *Fatima* (Milan, Italy: Ed. Paoline, 1979).

late Heart of Mary, I beseech Thee to convert the poor sinners."

The angel then stood up, took the chalice in his hands, gave the host to Lucia and made her cousins drink the contents of the chalice, saying: "Take and drink the body and blood of Jesus Christ who was horribly offended by the ingratitude of men. Make amends for their crimes and thus give consolation to thy God." He then prostrated himself on the ground again, repeated the same prayer three times and disappeared.

The angel never returned, he had performed his task. The children were now ready to open their hearts to heaven as it opened to them. As is common knowledge, this happened in the Spring of the following year 1917, at Cova da Iria, about three kilometers from Fatima, where Lucia's parents had a farm with a few oak and olive trees. It was precisely on one of these oaks that, on May 13th, there appeared to them She who Lucia described like this: "A Lady, dressed in a white that was brighter than the sun, emitting a light that was clearer and more intense than a cut-glass goblet full of crystal-clear water through which the strongest rays of the sun are shining . . . "

The three children were able to accept this visitation fearlessly because the angel had prepared them—accustomed to prodigies, they were ready to receive an even greater one.

●   ●   ●

The Virgin Mary also visited the village of Garabandal, near Santander in Spain. She appeared more than once between 1961 and 1965 to four children and performed many wondrous things. The Church has not yet pronounced on the events at Garabandal, but the

Madonna is said to have brought warning messages to these children and told them what to do. Her first visit was in October 1961, and one of the children, a girl called Conchita, was instructed as follows: "You must make many sacrifices and do many penances. You should be more assiduous in attending the Holy Sacrament. But, above all, you must be very good. If you are not, you will be punished. Your chalice is already filling. If you do not mend your ways, your chastisement will be great."

The second message came four years later and was brought by the Archangel Michael who repeated what had been said the first time and added: "I, your Mother, by the intercession of St. Michael Archangel, bid you to mend your ways. . . . Pray with sincerity, and whatever you ask for shall be granted . . . "

Once again, an angel had mediated between the human and the divine, between these children and the Celestial Mother.

Chapter 6

Emanuel Swedenborg's Angels

We have so far been considering angels as reported from orthodox sources—the Bible and the most reliable Christian traditions—and discerned the part played in their appearances by a celestial guardian. When we turn our attention from these undisputed sources to others that are less well known, and thus perhaps not officially accepted, we find further poignant and intriguing evidence about angels. Certain references and suggestions for further reading seemed to merit more attention and will be discussed in some of the chapters that follow. For now, we begin with a singular and very well-known figure who lived three centuries ago—Emanuel Swedenborg.

There is probably no other author in literature who has dealt with angels (and devils, too!) at so great a length or in such precise detail. Before quoting from the writings of this Swedish mystic and clairvoyant, it is appropriate to say a word or two about Swedenborg himself.

He was born in Stockholm in 1688, and can certainly be considered one of the most original spirits of his country and the whole of 18th-century Europe. The son of a Protestant Bishop, he was brought up in a deeply religious family atmosphere. He studied poetry, languages, literature and music at Uppsala University. Later on, his interest turned to science and he lived in England for a considerable time, where contemporary science was developing much more rapidly than in his native Sweden. He was a pupil of Newton, Halley, and the leading scientists of the day, and then went on to complete his education in Leyden, Amsterdam, and Paris. When he returned home at 26 his knowledge was encyclopaedic, and he brought with him sketches and plans for technical and mechanical inventions, with the intention of developing them in his native land. He had sketches of pumps, furnaces, cranes, mining instruments, aids to inland navigation, instruments of war and coastal defense, a military submarine and even an airplane. This, like many of his other schemes, became reality and in 1897 he actually succeeded in flying for a few miles. A model of his aircraft is still preserved at the Smithsonian Science Museum in Washington, D.C.

Swedenborg soon attracted the attention of the young and talented Swedish King, Charles XII, who appointed him "Extraordinary" Assessor at the Royal Board of Mines and helped him develop many of his projects. For thirty years he devoted his life tirelessly to science, researching and experimenting all over Europe. He published reports and treatises, and met the greatest scientists and thinkers of the time. He published as many as one hundred and fifty scientific works embracing every field of knowledge including mathematics, mineralogy, chemistry, astronomy, anatomy, and psychology. His studies constituted a carefully planned progression from the mineral kingdom to that of plants, then to the physical and subsequently psychological aspects of human beings.

For almost forty years, his scientific interests had prevailed over his religious interests, or rather, he had paid no further attention to religion. He continued to believe in God the Creator, but the mystical zeal of his youth had died down and he put aside anything that did not concern science.

It was at the age of 56 that his crisis came. He was now famous, but still with an insatiable thirst for knowledge. In order to find out more about the human psyche, he became one of the first to investigate dreams—his own—which began to get more and more strange, and provided him with new insight and paths to pursue. Dreams were followed by visions that revealed his new mission—to discover the hidden meaning of the Scriptures and describe the world of the spirit, heaven, hell and their inhabitants to mankind. From that day, angels and spirits were his teachers. Swedenborg became able to converse with people from the most remote times and be simultaneously a citizen of both heaven and earth. He visited extraterrestrial worlds in spirit and, immediately afterward, recorded everything he had seen in a kind of automatic script. The resulting works were highly original and have had great influence on personages such as Kant, Goethe and Jung. The poet Elizabeth Barret Browning said of him that in her judgment the only light we possess on the other life is to be found in the philosophy of Swedenborg.

The most detailed description of heaven and those who dwell there is found in the best-known of Swedenborg's works, *Heaven and Hell* which is a veritable vade mecum of the beyond. He has a lot to say here about angels, and the first thing he lets us know is that: "The angelic form is in every respect human: that angels have faces, eyes, ears, breasts, arms, hands and feet;

that they see, hear, and converse with each other, and, in a word, that no external attribute of man is wanting, except the material body. I have seen them in their own light, which exceeds by many degrees, the noon-day light of the world. . . . " He goes on to specify that: "angels cannot be seen by man with his bodily eyes, but only with the eyes of the spirit which is within him, because all the bodily organs are in the natural world, but the spirit is in the spiritual world, and like sees like, because its vision is from a like origin."[1]

To fully understand the angelic personages described by Swedenborg, we need first to have an idea of his conception of the extraterrestrial world and the life that awaits us after death.

He maintains that, after death, we do not find ourselves immediately in the life that is destined to us, but undergo an important process of transition. Immediately after we have made the crossing, we find ourselves in what he describes as the "kingdom of the Spirits," which is not yet either heaven or hell. We should never forget that Swedenborg used the terminology of his time and therefore tells us that heaven and hell are "states," rather than places. In the world of the spirits, people who have completed their earthly existence are taken care of and attended to. Certain spirits are, in fact, charged with the duty of receiving the new arrivals and helping them get used to the extraterrestrial dimension. They perform this task with great delicacy, granting the new arrival complete freedom. Above all, they transmit a feeling of great love and make the new arrival aware of the presence of a friend, someone who knows and can explain everything.

---

[1]Emanuel Swedenborg, *Heaven and Hell* (New York: American Swedenborg Printing and Publishing Society, 1859), § 75, 76.

In the other dimension, Swedenborg says, we pass through three stages: the first is that just described, i.e., the one in which the person who has crossed over emerges in the world of the spirits, is recognized, welcomed, and consoled. This state does not appear to last very long. It does not take long for us to become our real selves by a process of interiorization that manifests our real nature and true desires. On the basis of this, we begin to act as we really are. In the kingdom of the spirits, as I have said, there is great freedom and, for good or ill, everyone lives according to his or her own inclinations. This is what is meant by the judgment: God, who is pure love, does not condemn anyone, but everyone directs His own will toward one of the innumerable celestial or infernal societies. And in His love, God gives each person the right to do evil, otherwise he or she would be just a robot, unable to establish a pact of reciprocal alliance with God.

The final choice is made independently—and this is the third, definitive, state. Anyone who has chosen good becomes an angel and, like a chrysalis, sprouts wings. Those who have chosen evil become devils.

Here, now, are some of the things Swedenborg says about the clothing, dwelling places, and activities of angels. I can give only a few short extracts, and refer those interested to the much longer and exhaustive descriptions in *Heaven and Hell*.

> Since angels are men, and live together in society like men on earth, therefore they have garments, houses, and other things of the same kind, but with this difference, that they are all more perfect, because angels exist in a more perfect state; for as angelic wisdom exceeds human wisdom so greatly as to be ineffable, so

all things which the angels perceive and which are visible before them, exceed earthly things, because they correspond to their wisdom.

The garments with which the angels are clothed . . . correspond to their intelligence, therefore all in heaven appear clothed according to their intelligence; and because some exceed others in intelligence, therefore they are more beautifully clad. The most intelligent have garments which glitter as with flame, and some are resplendent as with light; while the less intelligent have garments of clear or opaque white without splendour, and the still less intelligent have garments of various colours; but the angels of the inmost [i.e., the loftiest] heaven are naked. . . . because they are in innocence and innocence corresponds to nakedness.[2]

Swedenborg, who really was a citizen of both Earth and Heaven, visited the heavenly regions during his visions and then described what he had seen. Here, for example, is what he has to say about the dwelling places:

I have seen palaces in heaven magnificent beyond description. Their upper parts were refulgent as if they were pure gold, and their lower parts as if they were precious stones: some were more splendid than others, and the splendour without was equalled by the magnificence within. The apartments were ornamented with decorations, which neither lan-

---

[2]Emanuel Swedenborg, *Heaven and Hell* (New York: American Swedenborg Printing and Publishing Society, 1859), § 177, 178, 179.

guage nor science can adequately describe. On the south were paradises, in which all things were similarly resplendent; for in some places the leaves of the trees were like silver and the fruits like gold. . . . The angels said that such things and innumerable others still more perfect, are presented before their eyes by the Lord, but that nevertheless they delight their minds more than their eyes, because in everything they see correspondences, and by correspondences, things divine.

I have also been informed [by the angels] that not only the palaces and houses, but the minutest particulars both within and without them, correspond to interior things which are in the angels from the Lord; that an entire house corresponds to their good, and the various things within it to the various particulars of which their good is composed; and that all things out of the house correspond to their truths which are derived from good, and also to their perceptions and knowledges. . . . The houses in which the angels live are not built like houses in the world; but are given them freely by the Lord, according to their reception of good and truth.[3]

Concerning the innumerable activities and tasks of the angels, Swedenborg says, the societies of angels in heaven are distinguished by their activities and customs. There are some societies that take care of the little children; others teach them when they grow up; others foster the simple and good in the Christian world and

---

[3]Emanuel Swedenborg, *Heaven and Hell*, § 185, 186, 189.

lead them toward Heaven; still others protect them
from the manifestations of evil spirits, which are
apprentice spirits that have just arrived from the Earth;
others check on those that are in Hell, and moderate
them so that they do not torment each other beyond the
prescribed limits. Swedenborg also says that angels of
all societies are sent among people to protect them
against erroneous thoughts and desires. If they are
received freely, they send them good feelings that help
them to repel evil intention. All these functions are
functions of the Lord performed by the angels, because
the angels perform them not for themselves, but on the
basis of the divine order.[4]

When reading Swedenborg, one thing should be
kept in mind; he well knew that it is impossible to
describe the phenomena of the spiritual world as they
really are, but only through images taken from the
world and human concepts. What he has to say about
the "peace of Heaven," which I quote below, is valid in
the last analysis for all descriptions of the life beyond,
and in particular for the angelic beings to which he
devotes so much of his treatise:

"No one who has not been in the actual enjoyment
of the peace of heaven, can have any perception of what
the peace is in which the angels exist. For man, so long
as he remains in the body, cannot receive the peace of
heaven, consequently, cannot have perception of it,
because the seat of his perceptions is in his natural man.
In order to his having a perception of the peace of
heaven, it is necessary that his state should be such, as
to admit of his being elevated and withdrawn, as to his

---

[4]Emanuel Swedenborg, *Heaven and Hell*, § 391.

Plate 17 (previous page). "The Ascent to the Empyrian" by Hieronymus Bosch (Venice, Doge's Palace). Bosch, who lived in Holland from 1450 to 1516, drew the inspiration for his art from popular magical, occult, and religious themes. This famous painting is his most faithful and impressive representation of what dying people see (see chapter 7 on this subject). We find ourselves in a dark tunnel that leads to a dazzling light, and the souls that make the crossing are escorted by their guardian angels.

Plate 18 and 19. Angels as musicians. This particularly stimulating work is preserved in the Fine Arts Museum in Antwerp. A detail of a panel by Hans Memlinc, 15th century.

Plate 20. Angels shown as children busy hunting. "Putti," or angelic children, first appear in Greek mythology as companions of Eros and Dionysius. They were later adopted by Christianity. This delightful painting is preserved in the Bardo Museum at Tunis.

Plate 21. Angels as musicians. The work of Baldassare Franceschini, known as "il Volterrano" (1644). They adorn the ceiling and lunettes of the Grassi Chapel in the SS Annunziata in Florence.

Plate 22. Beato Angelico: "The Coronation of the Virgin." Uffizi Gallery, Florence (detail from the left side showing angels and saints).

110

Plate 23. Beato Angelico: "The Cortona Annunciation," Museo del Gesù (the Angel Gabriel). Beato Angelico was particularly fond of the figure of the "Protector" who is loftily and poetically represented in a number of his paintings.

Plate 24. In the pack of tarot cards designed by Oswald Wirth angels appear frequently to illustrate a variety of different situations and contexts.

thought, from the body, and kept in the spirit, and being, when in the spirit, in the company with angels.[5]

As well as a language, Swedenborg says that the angels have a written script that corresponds to their wisdom and knowledge and is unintelligible to humans. Their writing has a literal sense and an inner or spiritual sense, and it derives directly from their thought. Those who have no knowledge of Heaven and see it purely as an atmosphere in which angels flutter as ethereal beings, cannot conceive that there may exist a language and a script. They place the existence of all things only in the material world, but the things in Heaven exist and are real exactly as those of the world; and in Heaven the angels have everything that serves their life and wisdom.

This is what Swedenborg has to say about the wisdom of the angels, which derives from their living in the Divine light: "The nature of the wisdom of the angels cannot be described by words; it can only be illustrated by some general facts belonging to it. Angels can express in one word what man cannot do in a thousand; and besides this, there are comprised in one word of angelic language innumerable things, which cannot be expressed in the words of human language at all; for in every one of the words uttered by angels there are arcana of wisdom in continuous connection, beyond what human sciences can ever read."[6] Swedenborg goes on to say that the wisdom of the angels is continuously improving, and may do so unto eternity, because wisdom is divine and infinite, while that of the angels is finite. And there is no comparison between infinite and finite.

---

[5]Emanuel Swedenborg, *Heaven and Hell*, § 284.
[6]Emanuel Swedenborg, *Heaven and Hell*, § 269.

In *Heaven and Hell*, Swedenborg says countless things about the life of the angels, their occupations, tasks, desires and hopes. He also says that they are sexed, and so divided into male and female. Consequently, there is also marriage in Heaven, which is the joining of two souls into one, as willed by the Lord and corresponding to the union of intellect and will, good and truth. They take place between similars and are celebrated and feasted in Heaven according to their own customs. These marriages, Swedenborg says, should not be called weddings, but fusions of souls through the union of good and truth.

What emerges is a most dynamic vision of the beyond, where it is possible—as we have seen—to evolve, make independent and personal choices, and grow in wisdom and love. This "beyond" is very distant from certain static preconceptions and one which, to a great extent, satisfies our expectations as active human beings alien from all kinds of immobility.

Among the many tasks of the angels there is, as we already know, also that of following humans during their lives and trying to influence them positively— always respecting their individual freedom. The same applies to the devils, but in reverse: they try to influence people negatively, to induce them to choose evil, both during their lives and after they are dead. Freedom lies precisely in this double and opposite influence, in that people are free to choose one or the other, both when alive and dead. Man is linked to Hell by evil spirits living in the world of spirits, and to Heaven by the good spirits in the same world. It is from this that proceeds the freedom of man. Swedenborg thus maintains that there is a continuous union between our world and the extraterrestrial, a union made possible because we are citizens of the world and also potential citizens of Heaven.[7]

Emanuel Swedenborg's angels were not created in the beginning, but gradually brought into existence as human beings returned to the Father. In Heaven—he writes—are those who lived out in the world a heavenly love and faith. But those who lived out an infernal love and an infernal faith are in Hell. All of them, angels and devils, must at some time have begun their life on earth, or on one of the innumerable planets of the universe. In the other dimension they then continued to evolve and either reached Heaven or became one with Hell.[8]

It is obviously not easy to summarize briefly what Swedenborg has said in hundreds of stimulating pages. However we consider it, his thinking has had—and continues to have—great influence, and is undoubtedly a strong encouragement for us to assume the responsibility of our own moral attitude and behavior, because it is these alone that shape our future destiny and can turn us into angels of light or abysmal devils.

---

[7]Emanuel Swedenborg, *Heaven and Hell*. See § 292 ff.
[8]Emanuel Swedenborg, *Heaven and Hell*. See § 291–302.

Figure 4. An angel blowing the Fourth Trumpet, from Douce Apocalypse, Bodleian Library, 13th century.

Chapter 7

Beings of Light

The Roman Catholic Church teaches that each of us has a guardian angel who protects and watches over us. This is reflected in the prayer all Catholics learned as children:

Angel of God who are my guardian
enlighten, watch over, support and rule me,
who was entrusted to you by the heavenly piety.
Amen.

St. Thomas Aquinas, in his *Summa Theologiæ* reaffirms this ancient teaching and confirms that we all have a guardian angel close to us throughout our lives.[1] It helps us cross over to the beyond, indicating the place to which we are destined. On this last point Tertullian, too, a Father of the Church, expresses himself in the same terms, affirming that when the soul is reawakened after crossing over it jumps for joy at the sight of the face of its own angel who is preparing to lead it to its new dwelling place.

---

[1]St. Thomas Aquinas, *Summa Theologiæ* (New York and London: McGraw-Hill and Eyre of Spottiswoode, 1968).

There is considerable modern evidence that seems to confirm this very early belief. I refer to the visions of dying people, i.e., that of those who were in coma, or at least at the point of death, and saw and felt—in that no-man's-land between here and the beyond—something that remained indelibly engraved on their memories. From all parts of the world, thousands of such experiences have been collected and their agreement—making due allowance for the considerable social and cultural differences and religious expectations of the protagonists—is one of the factors that leads us to believe that they are something more than dreams or visions.

The typical aspects of such near-death experiences are as follows: once wakeful consciousness has been extinguished, the people find themselves outside their own bodies, deprived of their material shell, but perfectly capable of thinking, remembering, seeing, and feeling. They perceive everything that is taking place around the inanimate body, but cannot convey this to those present. Simultaneously, they are in contact with another, different and superior dimension that everyone who has experienced it defines as extraterrestrial. They all see marvelous landscapes, hear very harmonious music and, above all, find themselves bathed in an extraordinary light, which they all say is indescribable in human words. The word that best approaches this new dimension and light is love.

Some of them also see a film of their lives in which they see again the whole of their past, and make an ethical judgment on it. Others say they meet a "being of light," who plays a part very similar to that of a guardian angel.

In one of her books on the experiences of dying people Dr. Elisabeth Kübler-Ross, one of the pioneers of these studies, said that the Church tells small children about guardian angels in the belief that each of us is accompanied from birth to death by spiritual beings. We all have these escorts, whether we believe it or not, and whether we are Jewish, or Catholic, or profess no religion; and our own personal beliefs are of no importance. Because universal love is unconditioned and boundless, everyone receives this gift at birth. Children often call their escorts imaginary friends and are perfectly aware of their presence.[2] When the time comes for them to go to school, though, adults see to it that they forget about these friends—until they are on their deathbeds. One old lady said to me, for example: "Look, he's back again!" When I asked her to tell me who "he" was, she answered: "When I was a small girl, *he* was always beside me. Then I completely forget about his existence." The next day the lady died happily because someone who knew all about boundless love was there, waiting for her.

In his well-known book *Life after Life*, the American doctor Raymond A. Moody writes: "What is perhaps the most incredible common element in the accounts I have studied, and is certainly the element which has the most profound effect upon the individual, is the encounter with a very bright light. Typically, at its first appearance this light is dim, but it rapidly gets brighter until it reaches an unearthly brilliance. Yet, even though this light . . . is of an indescribable brilliance, many make the specific point that it does not in any way hurt their eyes or dazzle them, or keep them from seeing other things around them (perhaps because at this point they don't have physical 'eyes' to be dazzled).

---

[2]See the case of Giorgia, the little girl in chapter 12.

"Despite the light's unusual manifestation, however, not one person has expressed any doubt whatsoever that it was a being, a being of light. . . . The love and the warmth which emanate from this being to the dying person are utterly beyond words, and he feels completely surrounded by it and taken up in it, completely at ease and accepted in the presence of this being. He senses an irresistible magnetic attraction to this light. He is ineluctably drawn to it.

"Interestingly, while the above description of this being of light is utterly invariable, the identification of the being varies from individual to individual and seems to be largely a function of the religious background, training, or beliefs of the person involved. Thus, most of those who are Christians in training or belief identify the light as Christ and sometimes draw Biblical parallels in support of their interpretation. A Jewish man and woman identified the light as an 'angel'. . . . they took to be an emissary or a guide. . . . Shortly after its appearance, the being begins to communicate with the person who is passing over. . . . For, here again, people claim that they did not hear any physical voice or sounds coming from the being, nor did they respond to the being through audible sounds. Rather, it is reported that direct, unimpeded transfer of thoughts takes place, and in such a clear way that there is no possibility whatsoever either of misunderstanding or of lying to the light."[3]

[3]Raymond A. Moody, Life After Life (New York: Bantam Books; London: Corgi, 1975), pp. 58–60.

From the many experiences Moody reports in his book, here is one that sums up all the rest:

"I knew I was dying and that there was nothing I could do about it, because no one could hear me. . . . I was out of my body, there's no doubt about it, because I could see my own body there on the operating room table. My soul was out! All this made me feel very bad at first, but then, this really bright light came. It did seem that it was a little dim at first, but then it was this huge beam. It was just a tremendous amount of light, nothing like a big bright flashlight, it was just too much light. And it gave off heat to me, I felt a very warm sensation. . . . It seemed that it [the light] covered everything, yet it didn't prevent me from seeing everything around me—the operating room, the doctors and nurses, everything. I could see clearly, and it wasn't blinding. . . . then it asked me if I was ready to die. It was like talking to a person, but a person wasn't there. The light's what was talking to me, but in a *voice*.

"Now I think that the voice that was talking to me actually realized that I wasn't ready to die. You know, it was just kind of testing me more than anything else. Yet, from the moment the light spoke to me, I felt really good—secure and loved. The love which came from it is just unimaginable, indescribable. It was a fun person to be with! And it had a sense of humor, too—definitely!"[4]

In another, more recent, book on near-death experiences, *The Light Beyond*, Dr. Moody pays attention to a particular group of cases, that of children.[5] What they

---

[4]Raymond A. Moody, *Life After Life* (New York: Bantam Books; London: Corgi, 1975), pp. 63–64.
[5]Raymond A. Moody, *The Light Beyond*, (New York: Bantam Books, 1989).

see when close to death is highly significant because they have not experienced the social and cultural conditioning of adults and are thus free from them. Moody discovered that their experiences are similar to those of adults: the feeling that they were outside the body, panoramic visions of their lives, the tunnel, meeting with relatives who had already died and with a being of light, and return to the body.

The first case Dr. Moody deals with is that of a boy of 9, called Sam, who nearly died of an illness. Sam told him that he saw himself outside his body looking down from a height on the doctor who was doing his best to reanimate him. He then climbed upward, passed through a dark passage and met a group of extremely luminous *wingless angels*, who seemed to be very fond of him. There was a magnificent light there where he found himself and he would willingly have stayed, but a being of light ordered him to go back and enter his body again. According to Sam, that being was God.

The meeting with beings of light that those who have been reanimated so frequently say took place has a special significance. It brings calm and reassurance, and remains impressed on their minds for the whole of their lives. Dr. Moody also reports that he spoke to an adult who had a near-death experience as a child which freed him from the fear of dying. Later in life he was twice in danger of dying, the second time after he had been kidnapped. But he was not really afraid because the memory of the being of light was a comfort to him and gave him immense peace and reassurance.

Another boy, called Jason, had been run over by a car and given up for dead. Later, the doctors succeeded in reanimating him. He had watched while they tried to bring him back to life and then found himself in a tunnel with a great light at the end of it. While he went along it, climbing higher and higher, he realized that he was being escorted by "two people." During the crossing, these two people had given him love and reassured him that they would take care of him and bring him to the light. They were dressed in white and extremely luminous. It was these two beings of light who told Jason that he must return to Earth, his parents and his sister, because his moment had not yet come.

They escorted him down the tunnel again, and he found himself back in his body. He knew that he would recover, and completely lost the fear of dying. He said that he had learned that the most important thing in life is love.

In several other of the cases Dr. Moody reports, children meet a being of light who asks them if they prefer to stay or return to earth; and they choose to return to see their mothers. The beings of light always agree with their decisions. Other researchers who have dealt with experiences at the point of death have recorded meetings with beings of light who play parts very similar to those of angels.

Kenneth Ring, Professor of Psychology at the University of Storrs, Connecticut, has conducted important investigations into near-death experiences. He, too, who has encountered hundreds of people who have had such experiences, has collected people's accounts of encounters with angels, which he writes about in his book.[6] As an example, here is a highly significant one that took place in 1954 to a young woman of 24. After her second childbirth (her baby was a girl) her life was in danger from a serious hemorrhage and respiratory problems.

------

[6]Kenneth Ring, *Heading Toward Omega: In Search of the Meaning of the Near-Death Experience* (New York: Quill, William Morrow, 1984).

Ann (this was her name) suddenly felt: ". . . a sense of being pulled (up! – not down) by some great force, out of the room toward a bright light, which seemed far away at first but I 'flew' toward it very swiftly. The pain fell behind me. . . . I suddenly stopped and felt myself lying perfectly still – like floating on water. . . . It was absolute – perfect – wonderful. I didn't know where I was, but I didn't care, I would be content to stay there *forever*! Then, 'I knew' he was on his way toward me from an unthinkable distance away. . . . He . . . came to me at an unthinkable high speed, passing through the universe. . . . I was in a world . . . of total nothingness, except myself. The bright light I had seen at first . . . was all about me now, but not bright anymore – soft now, and soothing. . . . I felt . . . very comfortable there.

She then felt that someone was approaching her. "And I 'knew' the exact instant he entered into the outer edge of the world (or state of awareness?) I was in. He came to me from my right-hand side. In a matter of seconds he entered 'my world' hundreds and thousands of light years away . . . traveled to my side and took hold of my right hand.

"When he took hold of my hand, I immediately knew him to be the greatest friend I had. I also knew that I was a very special person to him. The thrill of this touch of hands exceeds anything I have ever experienced on earth, in life as we know it. Our meeting was 'understood' – 'sensed' – not visual.

"Without vocal communication he 'told me' he had come for my child. '*My child*?' I asked, scarcely able to contain my joy and happiness over the news that one of my own children would be going back *with him*! It was, I 'knew,' a very high honor to be selected for this. I had the honor of being the mother of a very extra special child, and I was so proud that he had picked *my* child. (We were discussing her *life*, not death!) It was a fantastic opportunity for my child, and it never occurred to me to refuse to give my child to this man."

This 'man' stepped back so she could see the nurses, the doctor, and her baby, back in the delivery room. The doctor was examining the baby and laying it on a scale-like machine which was supposed to indicate its life-span (rather than weight!). She saw that the machine was malfunctioning and gave the doctor an incorrect reading. The doctor said the child would live 80 years. But the man with her said the machine was wrong, for the child would live only 4 days.

Ann wanted to know if the man would still take her child, and he agreed to return in 4 days. He let go of her hand and she fell away from him, moving downward quickly to return to consciousness to find the nurse calling her name and slapping her face. When she finally opened her eyes, the nurse showed her the baby girl. Ann heard that her own situation had been critical. She felt that there was something she was supposed to tell her physician about her baby—but she simply could not remember it.

Two days later the doctor detected severe cerebral hemorrhaging and on the morning of the fourth day the baby died. Ann was filled with joy, which no one could understand. Her husband had heard of other similar experiences from his patients although they were not called near-death experiences in 1954.

After Tari (the baby's name), Ann had three more children. Her husband died and her firstborn son was killed in a car accident. . . . "My grief was softened and shortened each time"—Ann wrote to Dr. Ring—"People said, 'She's in shock now, she'll grieve more later.' Later they said, 'She must be a very strong person to live through what she's had to live through so calmly.' Neither statement was true. It feels good to tell the truth to someone. They aren't dead. They are all alive, busy and waiting for me. Our separation is only temporary and very short compared to all of eternity.'"[7]

•   •   •

In the course of my own personal researches in Italy I also can report meetings with angels.[8] Here are two examples. The first was told to me by an Englishwoman, Mary T., who has been living in Naples for many years:

"In 1949 I had to undergo major surgery. I was tied down onto the operating table and the mask was put over my face for the anaesthetic. At the same time, at a signal from the anaesthetist, the nurse drove the needle of the syringe (full of pentothal?) into my left forearm. At that very moment, while I was still fully conscious, I thought: 'This is terrible! What I was thinking was that it was terrible to abandon oneself, in full consciousness and vitality, to death . . .

"At that moment, or perhaps a few seconds later, I felt a large, strong but gentle hand take hold of my right hand. . . . I was obliged to move and the hand led me. Meanwhile a man's voice that was serious but subdued, imperative yet protective at the same time, answered me: 'No, it's not terrible, come along, come, come . . .'

"It was the rather rough and serious voice of a grown man, but so reassuring and friendly that I went with him trusting and obeying. That hand led me,

---

[7]Kenneth Ring, *Heading Toward Omega: In Search of the Meaning of the Near-Death Experience* (New York: Quill, William Morrow, 1984), pp. 77–82.
[8]Paola Giovetti, *Qualcuno è tornato* (Rome: Armenia Editore, 1981 and 1988).

weightless and completely free of ties to the earth, in a wonderful ascent, in restful yet, at the same time, exhilarating darkness, in which I found myself, and recognized myself in a dimension already known to me, to a place where I was welcome.

"And I raised myself, led by my Guide, as if in flight from left to right. I knew where we were going, I felt that we had to reach something, a place, a great light—someone or something fatal, huge, exhilarating and anguished that was awaiting me, and knew me already.

"Without any further sound from his voice, my Guide continued to communicate with me (and I understood him perfectly!): 'See how easy it is? Don't be afraid, this has been granted to you, but don't tell anyone. No one would believe you.' Then, with redoubled and gentle authority he transmitted to me: 'But remember: order, order, order . . .' And I understood the word in the sense of moral fiber, a lifestyle.

"I woke up suddenly, as if a hand had let go of me, or at least that was how it seemed. I found myself in my hospital bed and it seemed that what had woken me was the immense, rhythmic and tumultuous beating of my heart, which seemed to repeat the solemn and gentle echo of the last word of my lost Guide: 'Order, order . . .'

"At this first awakening I was filled with well-being and gratitude, but also with infinite nostalgia. But for whom? For what? I was confused, but wide awake, and remained there for a long time attached to that dream (or only reality) which had invaded my soul and thoughts like something complete, true and right that I had rediscovered, seen again and lived again . . . and now had lost again.

"I have never been interested in or afraid of dreams, but all of this has remained fixed in my memory as something exceptional, and in the many years that have gone by it has never faded or disappeared. I was able to write it down almost at one go. . . . On that which happened to me I base my hopes and my expectations."

•   •   •

During my investigations in Italy I was able to gather another very special experience: that of a woman who had remained at death's door for a long time after trying to commit suicide. In this experience, much more dramatic than the rest and quite different in content, there is a "presence" acting as protector, who advises, encourages and from the very start accepts the protagonist totally. A guardian angel? One is inclined to think so. In any case, here is the story:

"Some years ago, after a series of disappointments, illnesses, misunderstandings in the family, and so on, I decided I wanted to die. Do not condemn us poor creatures who go as far as to make this horrible decision. Unless you have experienced the sufferings of such a situation and the motives that lead to it, you cannot understand.

"And so I tried to kill myself, but was saved in time: even if it seems absurd that there should have been time. When I recovered consciousness, the doctor in charge of the ward, who had looked after me from the start, said: 'I did everything I could, Madam, but did not perform a miracle. Your condition was desperate, and it was not I that saved you, not I! Someone sent you back here!'

"I found out later that I had been in a deep coma for five days. Did I reach the threshold? I think so. One thing I can say with certainty is that when someone is in coma he has a thousand experiences that are not dreams, or hallucinations. It really is a second life that draws us into a world similar to our own, with happenings that are fantastic, but possible. Dreams are often hazy and disconnected, but what I saw and heard was incredibly clear. Even now, years after, I can remember every detail of what I saw and heard.

"I don't know how long it was after my tragic gesture, but at a certain moment I was able to understand and think. I woke up knowing that I had done something to my own harm. But I didn't know whether I was alive or dead, and didn't remember either why or when I had done it.

"I came to in a world of silence. I felt that I had a body and a mind again. I don't know how, but was certain I wasn't dreaming, but consciously myself, with my thoughts, feelings, and sensations, from which, though, the worries of everyday life were excluded.

"I said I felt my body, but that's not quite right: I knew intuitively I had one. I could feel no physical pain, and so my body was light, restored. I was seemingly in good health. Nevertheless when, a few days later, I made contact with my surroundings again—that is, when I came out of my coma—I realized that the fact was that my body was being tortured by the drip tubes, catheters, etc., and thus, of course, painful.

"I gradually became aware that I was in a dark room that was gradually getting lighter, as if I were becoming used to the darkness and able to make out details that had previously not existed for me. I found that I was lying on a cold, pink marble slab, covered by a thin blanket. I could see myself, but not from above: I could see where I was from the point at which I was. . . . I knew I had a body because I could make it out under the blanket, but I felt so well that I did not have that sensation. It was my mind that was suffering from the whirl of thoughts that were disturbing me. I tried to make out if any sounds were to be heard, or if anyone was with me, but I was alone, desperately alone. I was waiting for something, anything. But just had to lie there in a state of mental anguish that grew and grew. I knew I was somewhere in a hospital, even though the room I was in, a sort of large and austere chapel, sumptuous in a way, even though empty, was nothing like a hospital room.

"At a certain moment I realized that a dazzling light had been turned on at my feet, to my right, near the large marble slab. From a fine gilded, old-fashioned lamp a very white light was shining onto me, only me, and I seemed to be absorbing that light. . . . I waited and waited in that unknown dimension and only the light of the lamp brought me any comfort.

"At a certain moment it seemed to me that in that light there was a face, a young, pale, man's illuminated face, with black eyes, that were severe but friendly and full of understanding. Those eyes were staring at me, staring. I was able to communicate mentally with that being, and he answered me, also mentally. We had a long, wordless conversation. Help! I beg you to help me, whoever you are! The face in the light replied that I was to keep calm, stay where I was and trust him. But I was afraid. Where was I? Was I alive or dead? The voice told me to keep quiet and calm.

"From somewhere I heard the sound of voices growing louder. Many voices, and they seemed to be having a discussion. I knew that on the floor above there was a room with a white ceiling, a sort of convent cell. In it, several black-cloaked figures were arguing; about me, I was sure of it. They were faceless figures, or else had hoods that covered their faces. They seemed to be friars. I could hear their words only as noises and my mind told me the meaning of what they were saying. I knew that I was on trial, accused of having committed a sin for which I must pay. I didn't yet know, though, whether I was alive or dead, and so I didn't know—and still don't know to this day—whether the decision would be to send me back on earth or down to hell. Some of the voices were defending me, but the majority were accusing me and one voice was particularly harsh and pitiless; it was a strong, loud voice, angrily asking for me to pay the full penalty.

"Suddenly a door banged loudly, and there was the sound of the feet of people running. The voices grew louder, especially one of them, the harsh one, worse and more imperious than ever. The spiral staircase that led to the floor above creaked under the weight of a crowd of people, dark figures, old and bent. They crowded round me. I had only just time to give a last, pleading look at the light and again knew there was hope for me. And, indeed, when the figures were on the point of carrying me off, they were prevented from coming any closer. I escaped from their clutches because the light blocked them. It was the light that absolved me and held them back. Perhaps it enlightened them about the mistake they were making. The reality was that the light had absolved me from the start; although judging me sternly, it kept on sending messages of hope. Yet, it was not a real absolution, the verdict of guilty had been pronounced, and I was left to suffer all that fear and bitterness through to the end.

"The cloaked figures then stopped, stepped back and I knew (how I've no idea) that I had been found not guilty. They were certainly going to send me back among the living. Was that the sentence I feared? Or was I afraid I might not have saved my soul, since to take one's life is a mortal sin? I have asked myself this question many times, but have never been able to give myself an answer. . . ."[9]

I have quoted almost the whole of this lady's long story because it seems to me to be particularly significant and interesting. This is certainly one of those cases in which the part played by the angelic figure emerges most clearly. I need to add that the experience did not correspond in any way to what the protagonist was expecting. She told me: "What I lived through was completely unexpected. My delusion with life was total, yet I was convinced that God would be generous enough to forgive me. I trusted that what I should find would be much better than what I was leaving, which was a complete disillusionment for me—but it wasn't like that although, in the end, there was a sort of absolution."

This lady had never even given a thought to the role of the "protectors." She abandoned herself totally to God's mercy. She really did have a great experience of this mercy, even though in ways she hadn't imagined and through a mediator she had not invoked. Which—for the purpose of our analysis—is much more important.

I conclude this chapter with a particularly mild and reassuring experience, even though the circumstances under which it occurred were painful. It concerns the death of a newborn baby. It is reported by Aniela Jaffé, who was a collaborator of C. G. Jung for many years, in

---

[9]This true story is from my research into near-death experiences and is used by permission.

her book *Apparitions and Precognition*,[10] the result of a most extensive investigation into spontaneous phenomena, promoted by Jung himself, and eventually analyzed by Dr. Jaffé. One woman had the following experience.

> It was a wonderful night, full of stars, when I looked out of the window. I could see everything clearly, right down to the village. Suddenly, next to our neighbors' cottage farther down the hill, I saw a great angel standing. He was nearly as tall as the house. In the morning we were told that a little boy came into the world there in the middle of the night but that by three o'clock in the morning he was already dead. The mother grieved very much at first, but when I told her that she and her child had been in the care of an angel that night, she was comforted.[11]

Jaffé adds that the Greek word *angelos* means messenger and represents a bridge between the temporal and the eternal. This vision brought comfort and gave a meaning to the death of a loved one.

All these considerably varying experiences have an important element in common—the significance of the meeting with an angel that brings comfort and hope to them all. This also confirms the ecclesiastical teaching according to which an angel comes to receive us at the moment of death.

---

[10]Aniela Jaffé, *Apparitions and Precognition: A Study from the Point of View of C. G. Jung's Analytical Psychology* (New Hyde Park, NY: University Books, 1963).
[11]Aniela Jaffé, *Apparitions and Precognition: A Study from the Point of View of C. G. Jung's Analytical Psychology*, p. 24.

Figure 5. Seraph on a
wheel. 19th century,
Adolphe N. Didron,
Christian Iconography.

Chapter 8

The Angel in Us

Is it possible to speak of angels from the psychological viewpoint? Can we conjecture a "meeting" at the psychic level with the angelic beings to whom, according to so many religious traditions, we are entrusted? Is it possible to get far enough down inside ourselves to meet these figures of masters and counselors and then bring their teachings back to the surface, to the light of consciousness? It would seem so. At least sometimes.

The outstanding and enlightened sage who was Carl Gustav Jung wrote in *Psychological Reflections*: "In each of us there is another we do not know. He speaks to us in dreams and tells us how differently he sees us from the way we see ourselves. When, therefore, we find ourselves in a difficult situation to which there is no solution, he can sometimes kindle a light that radically alters our attitude—the very attitude that led us into the difficult situation."[1]

He also says: "Together the patient and I address ourselves to the 2,000,000-year-old man that is in all of

---

[1]Carl Gustav Jung, *Psychological Reflections: A New Anthology of His Writings 1905–1961*, edited by Jolanda Jacobi & R.F.C. Hull (Princeton, NJ: Princeton University Press, 1970), p. 76 (45:325).

us. In the last analysis, most of our difficulties come from losing contact with our instincts, with the age-old unforgotten wisdom stored up in us."[2]

Dr. Jung speaks both on the basis of his experience of psychotherapy and his own personal experience. In the chapter Confrontation with the Unconscious of his autobiographical *Memories, Dreams, Reflections*, he tells how there emerges from his own unconscious an imaginary figure he calls Philemon, who appeared to him the first time as a tall old man with bulls' horns. "Philemon was a pagan and brought with him an Egypto-Hellenistic atmosphere with Gnostic coloration. His figure first appeared to me in the following dream. There was a blue sky, like the sea, covered not by clouds but by flat brown clods of earth. It looked as if the clods were breaking apart and the blue water of the sea was becoming visible between them. But the water was the blue sky. Suddenly there appeared from the right a winged being sailing across the sky. I saw that it was an old man with the horns of a bull. He held a bunch of four keys, one of which he clutched as if he were about to open a lock. He had the wings of the kingfisher with its characteristic colors."[3]

This dream image of Jung's is connected with a remarkable contemporary happening that increased its symbolical significance: "Since I did not understand this dream-image, I painted it in order to impress it upon my memory. During the days when I was occupied by the painting, I found in my garden, by the lake shore, a dead kingfisher! I was thunderstruck, for kingfishers are quite rare in the vicinity of Zürich and I have

---

[2]Carl Gustav Jung, *Psychological Reflections: A New Anthology of His Writings 1905–1961*, p. 76 (39H*).

[3]C. G. Jung, *Memories, Dreams, Reflections* (New York: Pantheon Books, 1961), pp. 182, 183.

never since found a dead one. The body was recently dead—at the most, two or three days—and showed no external injuries."[4]

As time passed, Philemon became more and more real and substantial, until he existed for Jung as a person with whom he was able to converse. Still in his *Reflections*, he said that Philemon and the other images of his imagination provided him with the decisive conviction that there are things in the psyche that are not produced by the ego, but produce themselves and have a life of their own. Philemon represented a force that was not Jung. In his imagination he held conversations with him and Philemon told him things that he had never consciously thought about. Philemon told Jung that he treated thoughts as if he produced them, himself, but Philemon said that thoughts have a life of their own. Philemon said, "If you should see people in a room, you would not think that you had made these people, or that you are responsible for them." In this way, Philemon taught Jung about psychic objectivity, the reality of the psyche. These talks helped Jung understand the difference between himself and the object of his thoughts. The meeting with Philemon convinced Jung that he was dealing with *someone* who had his own independence and autonomous wisdom. With an authentic master, in fact. He said that Philemon represented a superior intelligence. To Jung, Philemon was a mysterious figure. At times Jung thought Philemon was so real that he must be alive. He used to walk in the garden with Philemon who was what the Indians call a *guru* for Jung at different times.[5]

---

[4]C. G. Jung, *Memories, Dreams, Reflections,* p. 183.
[5]C. G. Jung, *Memories, Dreams, Reflections*, p. 183.

In reporting this experience of Jung's we certainly do not mean to claim that the great Swiss psychoanalyst had an angelic encounter. However, it cannot be denied that Philemon could represent a model which, from the psychological viewpoint, is reminiscent of the part played by angels.

•   •   •

A contemporary comparison with Jung's experience can be had from Dr. Eugene G. Jussek, a well-known and esteemed medical doctor who has treated some patients by hypnotic regression in order to bring to the surface traumata forgotten in childhood. While treating a young patient called Charles Roberts, who had psychological problems that were hard to explain, he brought to the surface memories of what appear to have been previous lives in England and Ireland. These memories were characterized by an immense amount of detail that Dr. Jussek was able to check. He was astonished to find it so accurate!

In the course of the therapy, another fact emerged that astonished the doctor even more: his patient seemed to remember a Being, a "person" who had always been beside him at the moment of death, and appeared to have the task of superintending the development of his soul. Under hypnosis, the patient called this person his "friend and master." Here is an example from the many that Jussek gives:

Question: After you died, what happened to your soul?

Answer: I was met by my wonderful friend. I do not know him by his name. He is ageless. Immediately after death we would speak of my experiences of that life-time and the lessons that were learned.

Question: Did you ask him about God?

Answer: It is always the same—that God is infinite.

Dr. Jussek was able to establish that this being appeared in his patient's memory every time he recalled the conclusion of a life. This naturally aroused his liveli-est interest and, in time, the doctor managed to get into direct contact with this "person" who said that his name was Yan Su Lu and that, to make himself mani-fest, he had assumed the personality he had had during his last incarnation (that of a Chinese sage who lived a thousand years ago). Yan Su Lu agreed to discuss fun-damental matters such as birth and death, reincarna-tion, suicide, the meaning of life, love, success and other things with Dr. Jussek. He added that he was Charles' guide and affirmed that each of us has a similar master and protector. From the extract that follows, which dates like the others from the late 70s, we can see the relationship between this figure of a master and counselor and guardian angels.

Question: What is a "guardian angel," do they exist?

Answer: We would rather not use the title "guardian angel," for as we discussed before, each individual in the incarnate state has many teachers. These teachers come to the individual for varying reasons. One would be for spiritual reasons, another for health, and another for, let us say, not exactly materialistic reasons, but to provide the individuals with the guidance to avail themselves the opportunity according to the pattern of their lifetime. But bear in mind each one of these teachers has in his own right, evolved to the level of spiritual being.[6]

In other words, he has learned much more than the individual he is with. It is true that these are guardians, but they do not interfere as that word might imply. To do so would usurp the free will of individuals. They are there for guidance and also to assist, when called upon, be it through meditation, or through prayer. They are there for this specific purpose.

The word "angel" was a title given to these teachers many centuries ago by the Christians who decided to put more emphasis on the spirituality of these beings. But the terminology is not completely true in that sense. These teachers do not have so-called "wings" which enable them to fly, not at all. They are their own individual spirit and conceive themselves in whatever manner they desire, but it would be in the etheric level.

Question: Does everyone have a teacher like Charles has you, Yan Su Lu?

Answer: Indeed. Throughout this universe teachers are with all living things. You must understand that the Father in His universal consciousness has appointed to all living things those who would guide and direct. These are teachers. In your religious connotations you would speak of them as "angels." We are here for all of you, to guide you in your hour of need, in your hour of meditation, in your hour of prayer. We are the ones who are there to respond to you in all ways that we can

---

[6]This concept coincides to a large extent with what Swedenborg says about angels. See chapter 6.

without, of course, interfering with your own free will and your own karma.[7]

•   •   •

Dr. Elisabeth Kübler-Ross, who we met in the previous chapter and may be considered the founder of modern research into death, wrote in her introduction to Dr. Jussek's book that she confirms what is reported in this book for it is substantiated by her own personal researches into life after death. The phenomena Dr. Jussek writes about are the same as those Dr. Kübler-Ross experienced in her twenty years of work with dying people. Spiritual masters are always near us and guide us from the moment of birth throughout our lives to the threshold we call death. They cannot interfere with free will—the most precious gift the Creator has given us—we are totally responsible for our decisions, actions, words and thoughts, says Dr. Kübler-Ross.[8]

In a conclusion to Dr. Jussek's book, the Rev. E. Stanton Maxey enthusiastically accepts this possibility of contact with the figure of a master who seems to exist in each one of us. And his invitation to readers seems to me to be the best way of concluding this chapter: "What can be said is that the possibility elucidated by Dr. Jussek's research is a gauntlet thrown down before each one of us. We may (must?) delve deep within our own beings seeking out our own Yan Su Lu. Such a quest augurs well the meaningful uncovering of hitherto un-

---

[7]Eugene Jussek, M.D., *Begegnung mit dem Weisen in uns* (Munich, Germany: Wilhelm Goldmann Verlag, 1986). From the unpublished English manuscript entitled *Encounter with the Wisdom Figure in Us: Conversations with Yan Su Lu*, mss. pp. 202–204.
[8]Eugene Jussek, *Encounter with the Wisdom Figure in Us: Conversations with Yan Su Lu*.

known spiritual elements within each one of us. The quest assures discovery. Only a short reflection upon certain events and dreams of this lifetime forces me to understand that no few of us have, are, and will encounter hierarchical spiritual beings who seek to guide our steps and enlighten our paths."[9]

We shall see in the chapters that follow that certain contemporary experiences, reported by people who are reliable and worthy of attention, seem to confirm the Reverend Maxey's hopes.

---

[9]Eugene Jussek, *Encounter with the Wisdom Figure in Us: Conversations with Yan Su Lu*, mss. p. 249.

PART
II

ANGELS
AMONG
US

Figure 6. Eros, a rose, a lyre, bring love to the world. Fifth century B.C., Etruscan, from the British Museum.

Chapter 9

Angels and Spirits of Nature

"Everywhere, all over the universe animate things are accompanied and guided by masters, because the Father in his infinite wisdom has placed beside every living creature those who can help and sustain them."[1] These are the words of Yan Su Lu, the Chinese sage we met in the previous chapter. According to him, then, every representative of the animate world is sustained and protected by invisible—but real—spiritual beings. Ancient writers were, in fact, firmly convinced of this and wrote about genii, elves, water sprites, spirits of nature, and *deva*.

In fairly recent times such spirits have been taken up again and extensively treated by a singular and most interesting personage: the Austrian philosopher and man of letters, Rudolf Steiner (1861–1925), the creator of anthroposophy, a theosophically-based doctrine which considers the universe to be an expression of the divine in continuous evolution, the purpose of which is to overcome every material obstacle and return consciously to

---

[1]Eugene Jussek, *Begegnung mit dem Weisen in uns* (Munich, Germany: Wilhelm Goldmann Verlag, 1986). This book is published in German and Italian; the title for the unpublished English manuscript is: *Encounter with the Wisdom Figure in Us: Conversations with Yan Su Lu*.

the divinity. Its origin can be traced to occult doctrines from the East, but it also includes Christian concepts, and tends toward a union of the two trends of thought.

In the vast, dynamic, and evolutionary concept of the universe he has outlined, Rudolf Steiner devotes a great deal of space to the angels and spirits of nature, which are the specific subject of his work: *The Spiritual Hierarchies and their Reflection in the Physical World: Zodiac, Planets, Cosmos.*[2]

In the first of these, he maintains that in order to speak of spiritual hierarchies we need our inner gaze to raise ourselves above human beings as they now live on Earth. Visible eyes can contemplate a scale of beings that represent only four levels of a hierarchy: the mineral, vegetable, animal, and human kingdoms. But above humans there begins a world of invisible beings and to humanity it is granted—thanks to a consciousness of what transcends the physical senses for as far as is possible to us—to rise a short way up toward the powers and entities that are the continuation, in the invisible and supersensory world, of the four levels that are found here on Earth.[3]

Steiner goes on to speak of the four elements—earth and water, air and fire: elemental spirits that live in the liquid and aerial elements and in solidified matter, beings to which we owe all that surrounds us, have descended from the fire element and are magically confined in the things we see around us.[4]

[2]Rudolf Steiner, *The Spiritual Hierarchies and their Reflection in the Physical World: Zodiac, Planets, Cosmos* (Hudson, NY: Anthroposophic Press, 1970).
[3]Rudolf Steiner, *The Spiritual Hierarchies and their Reflection in the Physical World: Zodiac, Planets, Cosmos*, p. 1.
[4]Rudolf Steiner, *The Spiritual Hierarchies and their Reflection in the Physical World: Zodiac, Planets, Cosmos*, p. 20.

These spirits, he says, make up the so-called lower world of the spiritual hierarchies. Then there are the angelical beings: first of all the angels themselves, invisible and immediately above human beings, messengers of the divine spiritual world. The archangels are two levels above us, and above them are the "spirits of personality," also called Principalities, primeval beginnings, or *archai*. These three ranks of beings who stand above humans, they were once human and have all passed through the human stage.[5] One can't help at this point thinking of Emanuel Swedenborg—who was the subject of chapter 6—according to whom both the angelic and daemonic kingdoms derive from humanity.

After the *archai* there are the Cherubim, Seraphim, and Thrones—all the result of evolution and the supreme hierarchy of divine beings who live closest to the godhead. Their activities are so sublime that human speech is inadequate to express them; these are spirits of supreme wisdom and infinite splendor.

But this is not all. Beyond them are the Dominions, Powers, and Mights. The last of these are also called Exusiai or "spirits of form." All together, these divine beings form a complex and perfect structure that gives stability to the universe, rules and preserves it.[6]

Steiner's ideas, which we have summarized as briefly as possible, are undoubtedly based on Dioynsius the Areopagite, but with the addition of Oriental elements. There are, for example, numerous references to the *Bhagavad-Gita*, the supreme Indian religious poem, and his own personal intuitions. His is an extremely

[5]Rudolf Steiner, *The Spiritual Hierarchies and their Reflection in the Physical World: Zodiac, Planets, Cosmos*, p. 31.
[6]Rudolf Steiner, *The Spiritual Hierarchies and their Reflection in the Physical World: Zodiac, Planets, Cosmos*. See chapters 4 and 5.

dynamic vision that allows us to glimpse a grandiose and endless cosmic path.

We shall be returning to Rudolf Steiner's spiritual hierarchies later, when we speak about Saul Bellow in our chapter on Angels in Art and Literature. We shall now stop to consider the spirits of nature, i.e., those natural forces – or beings – that preside over every manifestation of nature, take care of the growth of plants, regulate the watercourses and the blowing of the winds. They are manifest in will-o'-the-wisps, and are related to everything in the realms of nature that fructifies and matures. These creatures are innumerable, each with its own "territory" in one of the four elements. They are in close and direct contact with the "etheric body" of the Earth, i.e., the immaterial structure that is fundamental to every material manifestation. Steiner gave what has become a famous course of lectures on them in Helsinki in 1912.

Exactly fifty years after that course of lectures was delivered, in 1962, something happened in Scotland that seems to prove Rudolf Steiner right. Most people still tend to smile when the Scottish Community of Findhorn is mentioned, but those who know about it also know that it came to exist with the aid of the spiritual beings that preside over the growth and evolution of the entire world of nature. The founders of the community call them angels, or *deva*, which is the word the Indians use for angels. Let us take a closer look at the story of Findhorn.

●   ●   ●

Findhorn is a fishing village in the North of Scotland, a cold and windswept location. Yet, right there, a garden has grown as magnificent and luxuriant as you can possibly imagine—and it appears that we have the angels to thank for it!

"Yes, I talk with angels," writes Dorothy Maclean, a Canadian who, with her friends Eileen and Peter Caddy helped, quite by chance, to found the community: "great Beings whose lives infuse and create all of Nature. . . . I [never] imagined that such a contact would be possible or useful. Yet, when this communication began to occur, it did so in a way that I could not dispute."[7]

I was able to see for myself what Dorothy has written about when I visited Findhorn in 1987. In the middle of an expanse of cold and pebbly sand on the Scottish coast, there is a garden in which plants grow that have never been heard of in those latitudes either as regards their variety or vigor. A garden that has astonished soil experts and horticulturalists from all over the world, many of whom were unable to find any explanation for it within known methods of organic husbandry and eventually had to accept the unorthodox interpretation of angelic help.

After her marriage had failed, Dorothy Maclean was introduced to meditation by a friend called Sheena. It was Sheena who introduced her to Peter and Eileen Caddy and their three young children. They all went to Scotland and, in time, perhaps as a result of practicing meditation, something strange began to happen to Dorothy: when she was alone, she heard a voice that said: "Stop, listen; stop listen write."[8] She ignored the voice for as long as she could, but at a certain point it became so strong and insistent that she was forced to listen. This was how she began to write down very

---

[7]Dorothy Maclean, *To Hear the Angels Sing* (Hudson, NY: Lindisfarne Press, 1980), p. 3.
[8]Dorothy Maclean, *To Hear the Angels Sing*, p. 27.

beautiful messages, which were teaching her things that became more and more profound and enlightening.

After a great deal of doubt and uncertainty, Dorothy came to accept the reality and veracity of that Voice, which told her things she had never heard about, but which turned out to be right. Still today, Dorothy is receiving ideas and suggestions from her Voice.

She says she doesn't know who it is that dictates the messages to her, but is sure that it is not someone separate from her, but a voice she feels inside her and certainly cannot identify with anyone or call by name. It says things she would not be able to say, and helps her find satisfactory answers to many problems. She is convinced today that we can all hear this interior guide. It's enough to learn to listen silently, peacefully and trustingly.

Meanwhile Eileen, too, began to have the same experience and write messages that told her how to conduct her life and that of her family. The friendship between Dorothy and the Caddys was very close, also because they were working together. Peter was running a hotel in which Dorothy was the secretary/receptionist. Eileen stayed at home to look after her house and children, living a humble but happy life.

At a certain point, however, their problems began. The hotel closed down and our friends found themselves out of work and homeless, because they had been living in lodgings provided for them by the hotel. They had very little money, and so moved into the only place available to them: the Caddys' caravan (trailer) that was parked near the village of Findhorn. The site on which it was parked had no tourist attractions, but was functional, being situated on runways built by the RAF during the war. It was a cold and desolate spot, though, and they went to live there in bleak autumn weather.

Peter and Dorothy began to look for work, but were strangely unable to find any—and this was unusual because they were both well enough qualified to find jobs without much difficulty. Nevertheless, Dorothy and Eileen's interior guides reassured them that everything was going as it should, and that there was nothing to worry about. And so the Caddy family and Dorothy settled down to spend the winter at Findhorn, in the hope that the hotel would open again in the spring and provide them with work. But spring came round and there was still no sign of any work.

Dorothy writes that they needed food and Eileen's and her guides began to tell them that they must grow it by cultivating the soil. This was rather surprising because the place was absolutely desolate. But, in the ten years of conversation they had had with their spiritual guides, they had always been proved right, and this had not happened in vain. They therefore decided to make a kitchen garden beside the caravan. Peter, who had never seen a seed in his life, began to read books on gardening, but nowhere could he find any advice on how to grow things on sand. It was then that Dorothy had her great experience: her meeting with the angels!

Things happened like this: one day she began to get messages that were different from her usual ones. Her spiritual guide began to make new suggestions and indicate fresh paths. "One of the jobs for you . . . is to sense the Nature forces such as the wind, to perceive its essence and purpose for me, and to be positive and harmonise with that essence. It will not be as difficult as you immediately imagine because the beings of the forces . . . will be glad to feel a friendly power. All forces are to be felt into, even the sun, the moon, the sea, the trees, the very grass. All are part of my life. All is one life."[9]

On another occasion this was dictated: "Begin by thinking about the nature spirits . . . and tune into them. . . . They will be overjoyed to find some members of the human race eager for their help. . . . *In the new world to come* these realms will be open to humans—or I should say, human beings will be open to them. Just be open and seek into the glorious realms of Nature with sympathy and understanding, knowing that these beings are of the Light, willing to help but suspicious of humans and on the lookout for the false. Keep with me and they will not find it, and you will build towards the new."[10]

Dorothy was upset by these new messages; but her friends, the Caddys, encouraged her and she gradually succeeded in concentrating on the beings her guide had spoken of. It was thus that there began to arrive through the writings advice and messages from the "angels" (i.e., the spiritual Beings that preside over all the manifestations of nature). One of the first messages was this:

The duty of the spirits of Nature is: "to bring the force fields into manifestation regardless of obstacles, of which there are many in this man-infested world . . . While the vegetable kingdom holds no grudge against those it feeds, man takes what he can as a matter of course, giving no thanks, which makes us strangely hostile. . . . Humans generally don't seem to know where they are going, or why. If they did what power-

---

[9]Dorothy Maclean, *To Hear the Angels Sing,* p. 46.
[10]Dorothy Maclean, *To Hear the Angels Sing,* p. 47. Italics are mine.

houses they would be! If they were on a straight course, how we could cooperate with them!"[11]

Dorothy did not see angels, she simply felt their presence and wrote down what they conveyed to her. According to what they told her, they are energy fields, the intelligence at the basis of every species, the strength and energy that makes things grow. They are incarnations of the creative intelligence, vehicles for the expression of life at all levels. Their job is to promote evolution. Dorothy also found out that every species in nature has its angels, and she came into contact with those of the plants, becoming daily more and more convinced of the possibility of cooperating with them.

The collaboration came above all through Peter, who was struggling with his kitchen garden and encountering considerable difficulty with the soil. And so he prepared lists of questions which Dorothy put to the spirits of nature and received their answers and instructions. It was not long before she realized that it is only people's lack of trust that makes them decide certain things are impossible. She writes that, a little at a time, the spirits of nature taught them how to fertilize the earth; how to sow, how to treat each variety of grass, greens and vegetables, how to nourish them, when to gather them and how. As a result the garden began to prosper and give fruit. The angels also explained that the emanations radiated by the gardener contribute to the growth of plants, that the emotional forces that take care of the garden can become a real nourishment for the seedlings. Some people stimulate this growth, others hinder it, others even block it. Gar-

---

[11]Dorothy Maclean, *To Hear the Angels Sing* (Hudson, NY: Lindisfarne Press, 1980), pp. 48, 49.

dens, they insisted, are like children who need love and tenderness.

Here, to give you an idea of their quality, are a few of the many messages Dorothy received from the spirits of nature. The first dates to the beginning of contact and came from the Devas:

"Soar up with us and feel the bewitching strength of life's radiations as we know them. These are the radiations which we pour through the plants and which the plants bring to you. As you concentrate in peace and stretch your being up to these radiations, as you become sensitive to them on our level, you become more sensitive to them in the plants. Their essence is easier for you to touch on the inner planes with us leading you to them, but let our contact lead you to the outer world and let the outer lead you to the inner until all is one."[12]

Another very practical, yet at the same time poetic, message came to Dorothy from the "Landscape Angel." It was about rain.

She learned that rain passes through many radiations as part of a natural process, and it is far better for plants, than other kinds of watering. But when we do need to water, we can give out our own radiations which are almost as helpful as the natural ones that come with rain. When humans act as part of the "one life," they are transformers for many ranges of vibrations. The plants are grateful for the water given in such a way, and they are especially grateful for the love that is given with it.[13]

Another message came from the Deva of the lettuce plant. We can cooperate in many ways; the Devas con-

---

[12]The Findhorn Community, *The Findhorn Garden* (New York: HarperCollins, 1975), p. 80.
[13]The Findhorn Community, *The Findhorn Garden*, p. 81.

trol the life force in various plants. They can speed it up or slow it down. The Devas' work is not just setting the life force in action, and then letting the plants grow the best they can. They have been given certain powers, and within limits they wield them. The Devas will help us if we let them.[14]

The Apple Deva gave this Dorothy this explanation: "You feel drawn to us by the clustered blossom and the promise of fruit to come. That from a fragile, scarcely colored and shortlived bloom, a sturdy rosy apple appears, is but one of God's miracles enacted many times over for all to observe. If you could see more of how this is brought about by the chain of life, wonder would lift you high. . . . As from the seed a tree grows, so from the seed idea a pattern issues forth from the Centre, passed on by silent ranks of angels. . . . This is the word made flesh, this is all creation, held in balance by great layers of which your conscious mind is unaware. A miracle? You need a greater word, you need to go beyond words."[15]

Lastly, here is a very beautiful message from the "Lord of the Elements," the angel who presides over the manifestations of the wind, the sun, the earth and water—an invitation to human beings to get back in tune with nature, in the understanding that we are an integral part of it and aware that separation makes no sense because everything is part of God. He said we are children of the elements—composed of the elements. The world was made for us. Your bodies were made so we can express our joy in the Creator. But we are destroying ourselves because we think we are separate beings. The wind blows and it is part of us, and the sun

---

[14]The Findhorn Community, *The Findhorn Garden*, p. 82.
[15]The Findhorn Community, *The Findhorn Garden*, pp. 83, 84.

and water and air keep us alive. And when we suffer, the whole consciousness of Earth suffers as well as being happy when we are happy. This concept of oneness is everywhere. Oneness is not just on high or inner levels—where God is—but is here now. When people disturb the pattern of the Earth—the seasons—we are ruining the prospects for our future. We need to love life and join it. Life is part of the Creator, and all of life is also part of us.[16]

Dorothy Maclean and her friends Eileen and Peter Caddy accepted the reality of the contact with angels and spirits of nature and put into practice the teachings they were receiving, both at the personal and interior levels and the practical level, in work in the open air and contact with nature.

Little by little, the kitchen garden Peter planted on the sand became splendid and luxuriant—greens and vegetables of all kinds, herbs, flowers, blackberries, raspberries and strawberries. Later on fruit trees were planted that no one had ever been able to grow in the neighborhood—plums, cherries and apricots. As if that were not enough, the produce was gigantic—cabbages weighing twenty kilos, lettuces as big as cabbages, broccoli as tall as trees. Findhorn was transformed from a desolate waste into a magnificent garden, a Garden of Eden. It soon became news and soil experts came to visit from all over the British Isles. Not one of them was able to find a natural explanation for such an incredible crop having grown on arid, sandy soil without the use of pesticides or chemical fertilizers which the angels had expressly forbidden. The newspapers and radio began to speak of the "Findhorn phenomenon" with

---

[16]The Findhorn Community, *The Findhorn Garden*. See the complete text on p. 94.

the result that not only agronomists, but people from all over the world began to arrive, and some of them stayed to work with Dorothy and the Caddys. A small community grew up which increased over the years and developed into a school of life where people were taught and shown by example the right relationship with nature, one's neighbors and the Transcendent.

Everything at Findhorn began with the garden and contact with the angels that preside over the growth of every kind of life. The founders of the community had, at first, had no other intention than to provide themselves with food. But as time went by they began to understand that what was happening in their garden was for the purpose of showing the world that by collaborating with nature and its inherent forces it is possible to obtain incredible results even where to do so had seemed impossible.

Findhorn exists to teach us that we need to have a different approach to our planet. We generally think only of dominating and plundering it, instead of considering it as a living, palpitating creature with which a marvelous kind of alliance can be formed. The founders of Findhorn (and many thousands of people who have stayed in the community) are convinced that with love and goodwill everyone can do what they have done and make contact with the angels who are fundamental for the evolution of nature.

As I have already hinted, Findhorn is a school of life. The garden, which existed initially to attract the attention of the world, now grows more "normally." It is still luxuriant, but the produce has returned to being of the usual size. At Findhorn today they no longer limit themselves to agriculture, but tackle practical and spiritual problems. Lectures are given, courses of lessons and seminars, books and informative material are published. The garden is tended by everyone, on the same principles as the angels dictated to Dorothy Maclean, and many of the people I met at Findhorn say that they are able to "feel" the presence of the spirits of nature, and even to see them.

The aim at Findhorn is not to keep people there, but to train them. People of goodwill come from all over the world, are shown that it is possible to live healthily, to harmonize with nature and humanity, in tune with the spiritual dimension, and then return home transformed, to pass the word and show by example what they have learned and understood.

As Dorothy pointed out, if just three adults and three small children were able to create that marvelous garden, then if enough others got together in goodwill they could transform even the Sahara into an Eden. Anyone who has been to Findhorn does not have to make much of an effort to believe her right.

Who are we to thank for all this? The spirits of nature and angels who, once again at Findhorn, have sent a message to mankind—a message of cooperation, peace, and goodwill.

"We Watch Over the Earth"

Let us now look at an example of interior contact with the celestial protectors very near to us here in Italy. Elisa is a young woman of 35 who lives in Rome. She has practiced yoga and meditation, is a Christian but believes in the unity of all religions. Above all, she has faith in the interior God and has always believed in angels, because she, herself, has been in touch with them from childhood.

Elisa has no use for notoriety, all she cares about is that the messages she has been entrusted with by the angels should be known and accepted. "The angels," she says, "want it to be known that they exist and are anxious to help our planet to recover the equilibrium that has been upset. They, therefore, send warning messages to make us understand that we are all responsible for the Earth on which we live. They also say that in this epoch many people will have visions. They are, in fact, entrusting their messages of understanding to sensitive people who are implicit believers, able to open themselves to the superior dimensions."

Elisa's story and her contact with the angels is not all that different from that of Findhorn, at least on the ideal level and that of content and meaning. Unlike the protagonists of Findhorn who suddenly found themselves in contact with angelic beings and spirits of nature, Elisa has always felt the angels close to her and has even seen them: "They are tall, luminous, made of pure light and sexless," she says. "They have described themselves as 'beings of light vibrating in the Divine Energy, pure and uncontaminated by thought.' For as long as I can remember, before I fall asleep, I have always seen luminous forms near me who speak gently to me; I knew they were angels and was not afraid. At that time, on the contrary, I believed that it was quite normal to see angels, that it happened to everyone! Later, when I began to go to school, the angels helped me with my work, consoled me when I had problems, and were close to me all the time. In my teens, when I was at peace and relaxed, I also began to hear a voice speaking naturally to me and wrote down what it dictated. It spoke of heaven, the soul, and death as a crossing to another life. They were far superior to my powers of understanding and experience at the time, and I didn't say anything to anyone because I was afraid they would think I was trying to hoax them."

As in other cases of the kind, for Elisa, too, inner experience was not easy to achieve. It required a long journey over inaccessible territory. It was through yoga and meditation that she succeeded in leading a more serenely spiritual life and began to have genuine mystical visions of love and union with the All. The constant center of these experiences was always a meeting with the Beings of light, who Elisa felt to be permanently at her side and who, from 1987 on, have dictated messages to her about the future of the human race.

These Beings of light told Elisa this about themselves: "We do not consider ourselves to be weak, fragile, and wretched human beings, but shine with the divine gold that is in us. We are worthy Sons of the Father. He grants us the gift of sitting at His side, as the favorite Sons of the celestial Throne. We love what God loves, love God and God loves us. He has given us the universe to love, brothers to love, and the Earth to love. And this has given us a great heart that is the center of cosmic Love. We unite our minds and hearts to ask God the Father for peace in the cosmos to combat, and carry off like a river in flood, the wickedness and hatred in people. With our love, our prayers and meditation, we ask for enlightenment in our ignorance, love to replace hatred, and altruism instead of selfishness."

The angels speak to Elisa about their world which consists of levels and vibrations which, at our level of spirituality, we cannot reach. "The angels," she says, "urge me to arouse people's consciences and give them the messages. They invite them to love, pray, and think positively in contrast to the negative sort of thinking that has allowed human beings to pollute Earth. The angels need our collaboration. If we don't help them, they cannot operate for good. Their only aim is to realize the divine plan on Earth and in the universe, create harmony and equilibrium on our planet which is without it."

Among the many messages she has had from the angels, Elisa likes to quote one of 1985 that is particularly clear in purpose and intention: "We show ourselves to you brothers of the planet Earth, because this is a critical moment. There's no time to waste any longer. We have come to save your planet and need all the volunteers there are. We've no choice. In seven months there will be a tremendous cataclysm. Try to convert as many people as possible, speak of Christ and God and they'll believe you. We *watch over the Earth*. We are angels of salvation, each of us has a task. Purify your minds and hearts increasingly, fast, pray and convert."

The cataclysm the angels spoke of was Chernobyl. And that disaster did occur just seven months after Elisa received her message.

The angels also told Elisa that she had been trained for an important mission—telling people about their messages—for a twofold purpose: to let it be known that we are all responsible for the planet Earth over which it is the angels' duty to watch; and to set us on the spiritual path by providing sensitive and trusting people with knowledge. Elisa intends to take steps to have her messages more widely known in the future. And this book about the celestial messengers seems to be a highly suitable occasion for providing what can be only a fleeting anticipation of them.

Figure 7. St. Francis is believed to have become an angel. From a manuscript compiled in the 14th century by Jacobus de Voragine.

Chapter 10

Angelic Rescues

Even though, as theologians have pointed out, people seem to have forgotten about the angels, the angels—as is shown by certain exceptional witnesses—have not forgotten about us. Many people have told how they were "rescued" by someone they usually describe as being "young and tall, luminous and with a kind, attractive face." It is also typical that all these "young men" have disappeared immediately after they came to the rescue.

I admit that this chapter of my book on angels is decidedly "unorthodox," yet it did not seem right deliberately to omit such reassuring accounts. Many of the ones I shall include here involve lay men and women (although two exceptionally concern people in religious orders). It is, however, well known that such things happen to mystics and saints and, in fact, Santa Francesca Romana was saved by her guardian angel from the waters of the Tiber, and San Filippo Neri was literally lifted up by his angel, and thus rescued from being run over by four runaway horses and their carriage.

Why, then, shouldn't ordinary men and women glimpse the supernatural? Why shouldn't we believe in the possibility of miracles? Here, therefore, without comment or any attempt at judgment, are some examples of such events. The first concerns a Roman Catholic theologian, a German called Bernhard Overberg who lived in the 18th century. He was a renowned teacher for he reformed the scholastic system. He is unanimously described as having been an upright and well-balanced person and, in any case, witnesses have provided specific evidence that his experience was genuine. Here, in his own words, is what happened:

"One day I was seeing home a pair of nuns who, although they lived several days' journey away from me, had come to discuss important matters. On the way back, just as darkness was beginning to fall, we reached an expanse of moorland that extended all the way to N. (the town where the nuns lived). It meant another three hours' journey and, although our coachman was on the alert, he got lost and spent an hour trying unsuccessfully to find his way. And so, since the night was dark, we decided to ask for shelter in a farmhouse we happened to come across. The owners, a man and his wife, welcomed us very kindly and said they would be delighted to put all four of us up for the night. They served us supper. By the time we retired to our rooms it was after ten o'clock.

"While I was reading my breviary before settling down to sleep, the image of the angel I have always considered to be my guardian fell out of the book. As I mused for a moment or two on the good works angels performed there was a knock on my door. I went to open it and found a very handsome, well-dressed young man, who bowed before me and said: 'Sir, leave this house with the nuns before one o'clock, slip quietly out without making any noise. You'll understand why early tomorrow morning.' Having said this he left the room, leaving me absolutely astonished.

"It was then half past eleven. I looked again at the image of my saint and confirmed that the youth who had just visited me in that room was his look-alike. I hesitated no longer and went and woke the coachman, told him to get the horses ready quickly and quietly, and then woke the nuns. A few minutes later, we were all out of the house without anyone having noticed. Three hours later we got to N., woke the landlord of the inn where the coaches staged, and got the innkeeper's wife to make us some coffee.

"We had hardly sat down before a young commercial traveler rode up in great agitation, dismounted quickly and walked over to us. He sat down next to me, then jumped up and ran to the window, came back and sat down again, obviously extremely worried about something. When, in the end, I asked him to tell me why he was so upset, he made it clear that he preferred to speak to me in private. I signed to the nuns to leave us and, as soon as we were alone, he spoke as follows: 'Sir, what makes me so agitated is an incredible thing that happened to me in the night. A crime has certainly been committed! I needed to get to N. on business last night, but got lost on the moor and after wandering round for hours, reached a farmhouse. Because I had a lot of money on me, I didn't like to ask for hospitality for fear of being robbed. I rode round the house and saw a light in a back window. On looking in, I saw seven burly brutes of men seated round a table. Just at that moment, one of them looked at the clock and said to the others: 'It's one o'clock. The nuns and their escort are sure to be sound asleep by now. This is our chance!' They stood up and looked so menacing that I didn't wait for them to come outside, but rode off at a gallop, and here I am! I'm dead sure those men must have committed some sort of a crime!'

"I had realized from his description that his farm must have been the same where we had been welcomed so hospitably, and was very glad to be able to reassure him that the crime had not taken place because an angel had warned us and we had got away!"

•   •   •

Coming closer to our own time, here is another extraordinary case of a rescue. It happened during the second world war to the Rev. John G. Patton, a missionary in the New Hebrides. One night, according to his own story, the mission was surrounded by hostile natives who were clearly intending to burn it down and murder the pastor and his wife. Unable to defend themselves, the couple prayed to God for help. They were greatly surprised at first light next morning to discover that their assailants had disappeared without doing any of the things they seemed to have intended to.

A year later, the chief of the local tribe was converted to Christianity and the Rev. Patton, remembering what had happened that night, asked what had prevented the chief's men from killing him and his wife and destroying the mission. To his great surprise, the chief told him that while he and his men were getting ready to make their attack, they saw that the mission was guarded by a large number of tall, strong men dressed in shining clothes, with swords in their hands. This frightened them and so he and his men retreated and never went back to the mission because they expected to find it defended by those warriors.

The Rev. Patton is convinced (and he did not hesitate to put this in writing) that those figures who came to protect him and his wife and their mission were angels.

The next happening took place in China in 1942, after the Japanese had won the war against the Chinese. The story is told by Dr. Nelson Bell, who was working in the hospital at Tsingkiangpu, in the province of Kiangsu. He used to go to the Christian bookshop in Shanghai for bibles to distribute among his patients, and it was there that the story we are about to hear took place.

One morning at about nine o'clock, a Japanese truck half full of books stopped in front of the bookshop. There were five soldiers in it and the Chinese sales assistant of the shop, a Christian who was alone at the time, realized that the Japanese had come to requisition all the books in his shop. He was timid by nature and knew that it would be useless to try to resist.

The soldiers jumped down from their truck but, as they were walking toward the door of the shop, a smartly-dressed Chinese gentleman slipped in in front of them. The assistant did not recognize him and is sure he had never seen him before. For some unknown reason, the Japanese were unable to follow him in. They remained outside looking in through the four shop windows for two whole hours until eleven o'clock. Not one of them set foot inside the shop. The unknown customer asked the assistant what those men wanted, and he explained that the Japanese were emptying many of the bookshops in the town and that it must be his turn to be robbed. The unknown visitor reassured him and the two of them prayed together. The next two hours went by uneventfully and the Japanese soldiers got back into their truck and drove away. The unknown Chinese gentleman also disappeared, without buying anything or even inquiring about the books he had in stock.

Later, when the owner of the shop arrived, the assistant asked him: "Mr. Lee, do you believe in angels?"

"Of course I do!" Mr. Lee replied.

"So do I, then!" said the salesman.

When he heard the story firsthand from the salesman, Dr. Bell came to the same conclusion.

•   •   •

An Italian experience of the same kind is told by Mario. It happened in 1954, when Mario was 5 and living with his family in Naples. He used to play every day with a friend who lived in the same building, on the floor above. There were two flights of stairs to climb to get from one floor to the other.

One evening, while Mario was playing with his friend, he heard his mother call him down for supper. "As I was late," he says, "I ran to the top of the stairs, tripped and fell headlong, face down. But as I fell almost horizontally, instead of landing on my face, I felt a mysterious and irresistible force hold me up. I floated gently down. I could hardly believe what was happening, but it was wonderful—like dreaming I was flying! I went down the first flight like that, and when I reached the landing my body—still suspended in air—turned and flew down the second flight, too. Then I found myself *on my feet* in front of the door of our apartment. It must have lasted about fifteen seconds in all. All the way down it seemed that a force (or was it a pair of hands?) was keeping me up, holding onto my waist, as someone does who is teaching you to swim.

"Overcome with emotion, I rang the ball and, when Mummy came and opened the door, I shouted:

'Mummy, I flew!' But she took no notice at all, just told me to go and sit at the table!

"I am perfectly aware that I am unable to describe in detail everything I felt at that time. But from that moment, this wonderful and real event has remained in my heart and engraved on my memory. And every time I think about it I seem to relive the experience."

•   •   •

I conclude with a story told by Billy Graham, the American evangelist who has also written a book about angels. He relates that Dr. S. W. Mitchell, a well-known neurologist in Philadelphia, had gone to bed after an exceptionally tiring day, but was unexpectedly woken up again by a knocking at the door. When he opened it, there was a poorly-dressed and emotionally upset little girl who told him that her mother was very ill and wanted him to go and see her. It was a freezing-cold night and snowing but, exhausted though he was, the doctor got dressed and followed the little girl.

When they got to her home, they found the girl's mother in bed with pneumonia. The doctor did what he could for her, and phoned the hospital to arrange for her to be admitted the next morning. Before he left, he complimented the mother on the intelligence and good-ness of her daughter. The woman looked at him strangely and said sadly: "My daughter died a month ago!" She also said that her overcoat and shoes were still in the wardrobe there in that room.

Dr. Mitchell was astonished. He opened the ward-robe door and there, hanging up, was the overcoat the little girl had been wearing when she came and woke him up to tell him to hasten to her mother's bedside because she was ill. The coat was warm and dry, and could not have been worn by anyone that cold and snowy night.

Billy Graham, when he heard the story, immediately wondered whether in such an hour of need it was possible that an angel might have called on the doctor in the guise of the sick woman's daughter. Whether it actually was an angel, or the little girl herself, doesn't make much difference, does it?[17]

A Special Angelic Rescue

This very special experience was told me by a close friend, Dr. Dede Riva of Milan, whose speciality is psychodynamics. She works at a center for these studies, giving lectures and arranging seminars. This is what happened:

"Some years ago I heard that a very dear friend of mine had a liver tumor which had been diagnosed as malignant by a famous Milanese specialist. I felt that I had to do something to help her, and took her to Varese, to the home of another friend of mine—a pranotherapist and painter. She lives in a fine old tower in which she paints and practices. We held a pranotherapy session in a very serene and joyous atmosphere, which was strangely in contrast with the actual situation, since the patient had been given only two months to live. Despite this we felt inexplicably happy.

"After the session, as we were leaving the tower, we met two men, one about 5'6" tall and the other a little taller. One had a Slavonic-looking face and the

---

[17]Billy Graham, *Angels* (New York: Pocket Books, 1977).

other had finer features. They were very ordinarily dressed and spoke perfect Italian—but with an intonation that gave away the fact that they must have been foreigners. They stopped us and asked the way to a certain street, but we couldn't help because we didn't know the neighborhood. As we were beginning to walk away, my friend and I both turned round together and said: 'But, those two were angels!' And they had both disappeared.

"I do not know what made both me and my friend so certain that they were angels. But I do know we were sure—and I also know that my friend is still alive, in excellent health and that her tumor has disappeared without trace. I have no proof—only the precise and extremely vivid feeling that we had both met two special people. Perhaps it was the strange cadence to their speech, our inexplicable gaiety before meeting them, the radiation that came from them. Yes, all this together, and the fact that my friend is cured has convinced both of us that we met two protectors."

Dede Riva had no difficulty in accepting the idea that this was an angelic intervention, since she is not new to events of this sort.

"I have often had the feeling that someone was helping me," she says. "I'm rather timid by nature and often find myself in situations that are difficult to cope with. Ever since I was a small girl I have felt the presence of a protector. In those days I always tried to keep a place vacant for him next to me! And I still feel that he is always there and, whenever I need anything my thoughts turn to him, my guardian angel. It is thus that, at a certain moment, something happens to change my state of mind in explicably—I become different and know that 'somebody' is helping me!"

What comment is there to make about experiences of this kind? None, in my opinion. The best thing is to let the facts speak for themselves, and allow each story to have its own effect on us. As we shall see in the following chapter, there seem to be many more "angelic experiences" than we imagine. Perhaps all we need to do is ask, talk about them and have faith in them.

Figure 8. Sleep and Death carry a soul away. Detail is from a fifth century B.C. vase.

Chapter 11

An Angelic Quest

"What could have moved me in 1982 to start on a survey of experiences with angels? It was one of those impulses which cannot be explained logically. One day I was still living an ordinary life—to whatever extent life can be normal—and the next day I was in the midst of it all." This is how Dr. H.C. Moolenburgh, a Dutch dental surgeon, begins to tell the story of an unusual inquest that led him to ask 400 of his patients the not so ordinary question: "Have you, in your lifetime, ever seen an angel?"[1]

Dr. Moolenburgh was fascinated and at the same time embarrassed about his curiosity. In addition, he was fascinated by the way people answered him, for some were shocked, some were thrilled, some were delighted to talk about angels. When he came to study people's reactions, he found the following:

---

[1]H. C. Moolenburgh, *A Handbook of Angels* (Freiburg, Germany: Hermann Bauer Verlag, 1985). Published as *A Handbook of Angels* (Saffron Walden, Essex, UK: C. W. Daniel, 1988). Originally published by Ankh-Hermes in Holland, 1984.

65 people, i.e., 16 percent of those questioned, started to think seriously (a surprising result, in his judgment).

45 people (11 percent) had quite a different reaction. They burst out laughing: not into sarcastic or exaggerated laughter, but the peals of fresh, happy laughter that affirm without any doubt that such things just don't exist.

37 people (9 percent) were astonished.

Another 37 were greatly satisfied. It was the satisfaction of someone who finds unexpected confirmation of something he or she has already thought of.

19 people reacted negatively, becoming angry and bad-tempered.

9 claimed that they were already living with an angel: their own wife or husband.

Another 20 had a more constructive reaction: "No, I've never seen an angel, but . . . " and told him about an event that had to do with the world of the mysterious.[2]

Considering overall the reactions of the people he interviewed, Dr. Moolenburgh noticed that to the great majority (89 percent)—whether or not they were believers—the question did not seem banal and aroused an emotional reaction. And this information gave him the opportunity to make an interesting observation—that Western people are not as materialistic as we some-

---

[2]H. C. Moolenburgh, *A Handbook of Angels* (Saffron Walden, Essex, UK: C. W. Daniel, 1988), pp. 11–18.

times think. We live in a world where everything is
organized in a logical and rational way, but, if we look
below our rational veneer, we find that people are profoundly interested in the mysterious.

Before considering the practical results of our
search for angels, I shall quote the personal experience
with an angel of the man who started this search—Dr.
Moolenburgh himself. He reports, in his book on
angels, that one of the most beautiful things on earth is
the ever-changing sky, continuously crossed by many-
colored clouds and rainbows. He said that when he was
a boy, he was looking up at the sky: autumn was
approaching, he could smell the lighted fires, the
mushrooms, the dahlias in full bloom. The sky was
blue, except for a passing white cloud. While watching
the cloud, he saw a huge angel treading the sandhills by
the shore. His head was wrapped in a thin linen cloth—
the kind Arabs wear. The angel had just spread his
gossamer-light wings and was wearing a long cloak.
The sky around him seemed more vast and of a deeper
hue than usual—so blue that it was more like the sea.
Then the image slowly disappeared, and he went back
to contemplating his cloud. Did he really see an angel?
Did the wind chance to shape a cloud into a form that
looks like an angel?[3]

Let us now get back to Dr. Moolenburgh's search,
which may perhaps have been inspired by that long-
ago vision of an angel. Of the people he questioned, 31
(out of the 400 he talked with) said that they had personal encounters with angelical beings. Another 61 told
him of paranormal experiences and 7 reported near-
death experiences (they had been at the point of death
and at that moment had seen and heard things that had

---

[3]H. C. Moolenburgh, *A Handbook of Angels*, p. 39.

remained stamped on their memories). Here are some examples from his experience in Holland.

A young woman was in danger of dying after giving birth to a child. At night she saw a silver ladder leading up into the sky, and at the top of the ladder there was an angel who seemed to be waiting for her. She had only a moment to choose whether to go and meet him or return to her husband and son. She decided to return, and from then on she began to get better.

A fairly similar experience occurred to a man who, after a car accident, found himself in a hospital. He saw a brightly-lit door with an angelic figure in it beckoning to him. He felt such a strong desire to cross that threshold that he pulled out the intravenous needle that was feeding him. A moment later he reconsidered what he had done, thought it over and decided to come back to Earth.[4]

People see angels when their state of consciousness is altered, as in the two cases just reported, and also when they are normally aware and alert. For example, one man reports that he went to church one day with his fiancée. Suddenly they both saw near the altar a brilliant, but not blinding, light of a beauty that was supernatural. It was so strong that it completely blotted out the figure of the priest who was saying mass. While telling the story to Dr. Moolenburgh, this man became so moved that he began to cry. He insisted more than once that his fiancée had seen the same thing and that they both considered that experience as the most precious of all they had shared. The light had given them an immense feeling of peace and goodwill. Later on they asked the priest about it, but he had seen nothing.

---

[4]H. C. Moolenburgh, *A Handbook of Angels*, p. 24.

Plate 25. A fresco in Santa Cecilia, Rome. Franz Kafka (see chapter 13) had an exceptional meeting with an angel that appeared through the ceiling of his wretched rented room, filling it with its own radiant light, and may well have been not unlike this splendid Seraph. By Pietro Cavallini, 13th century.

Plate 26. "Angel with Ampullae" (1340), preserved in the Louvre, Paris. This altarpiece was commissioned by Joan of Evreux, for the Abbey Church at Mabuisson. It is attributed to Everard d'Orleans.

Plate 27 (opposite). A splendid polychrome "Annunciation" with flexibility of line. By the unknown author of an altarpiece (the "Altarpiece of the Life of the Virgin") preserved in Cologne Cathedral. Painted on wood, it dates to about 1360.

179

Plate 28. Shiva and Parvati, the divine bride and groom, represent the union of yin and yang, the two opposed forces of reality. Angels are regaling their masters with music and airborne dancing. An Indian watercolor from 1780.

Plate 29. A splendid "Annunciation" by Benvenuto di Giovanni (1470). Sinalunga, San Bernardino.

Plate 31. On its voyage beyond the earth, the soul must cross the river of the dead, and is able to do so only if it has acquired interior equilibrium. A very narrow bridge (judgment) separates the good souls from the bad. The good succeed in crossing and are received by an angel who escorts them to heaven. The sinners fall into the river and are swept down to the underworld. (Loreto Aprutino, a fresco in the Church of Santa Maria. A 13th-century illustration for Dante's *Divine Comedy*).

Plate 30 (opposite). The "Angel of the Annunciation" (14th century). This supple marble figure is preserved in the Metropolitan Museum of Art, New York.

183

وبعض ملائكه دكوغيب اولوب عبادتدن استكبار ايتمزلرنكه دنبا العزنت
بوردن من عندن لايستكبرون عن عبادته عندنه دنمراد قب شرقدر

Plate 33. The Prophet Mahomet, riding the mythical colt Buraq, is led by archangel Gabriel through the garden of Paradise, where dark-eyed Houris are enjoyably disporting themselves. A 15th-century work from Eastern Turkey, by Miraj Nameh. Islam shows the influence of the Old Testament by including in its pantheon numerous figures of angels.

Plate 32 (opposite). This 16th-century Turkish miniature shows angels performing rituals in heaven. According to tradition, Mahomet learned his Islamic prayers by imitating angels in paradise.

185

Plate 34. Gustav Doré, illustration to *The Divine Comedy*. In this exceptionally luminous representation, Dante and Beatrice are surrounded by hosts of angels. Engraving, 19th century.

Plate 35. Paradise is here represented as a rose garden. The part shown is the special Garden of Mary, Queen of the Angels. Mary herself is the most perfect intermediary between heaven and earth and therefore the Queen of the Winged Messengers. This work by Stefano da Zevio is preserved in the Castelvecchio at Verona.

Plate 36. Marc Chagal devotes a lot of space in his work to metaphysical, supernatural, symbolical, and dream figures. His skies are often inhabited by angels
and fantastic beasts in bizarre colors. Rather than in the artist's imagination, they
probably had their origin in a personal experience, described in chapter 13.

Plate 37 (opposite). The angels accompany the Christian tradition in the representation of the saints' lives, as well as in many stained glass windows.

Plate 38. The Earth belongs to humanity and heaven to God, but the ladder uniting them is in charge of the angels. This representation is from an 11th-century Anglo-Saxon manuscript in the British Museum, and shows Abraham prone on the ground before God, who has descended from heaven to promise him that he will be the forefather of a multitude of nations.

190

Plate 39. The Greek figure of *Nike* (Winged Victory) served as a model for Christian angels. This splendid stucco example was found in the gardens of the Farnesina Palace and is preserved in the National Museum, Rome.

Plate 40. This archangel happens to be Satan, who is considered to be accidently the cause of evil. William Blake here depicts the power, energy, loneliness, and glory of an archangel. Blake was a visionary painter and poet who believed himself to be guided by angels, and said that angelic messengers taught him how to paint. See chapter 13.

One of Dr. Moolenburgh's friends said that when he was going through a very difficult period, he was afraid he might die. One day, while speaking on the telephone, he unexpectedly saw the extraordinarily bright figure of an angel through the window. The angel spoke a few words of consolation to him, which later turned out to be providential, and disappeared.

One of Dr. Moolenburgh's patients told him about a childhood miracle when she lived in the country. A farmer lived close by and one day, her mother was told that the farmer's daughter was dying. The mother went straight round to see the child to pray for her. While they were praying, there was a loud knocking at the door. The mother opened the door and found a youth who asked: "What's happening here?"

She replied: "A little girl is dying."

The youth did not hesitate, but walked straight into the girl's room, put a hand on her forehead and cast out the illness in the name of Jesus Christ. He then walked out the back door and no one ever saw him again. This took place in the country where everyone knows everyone else, but no one there had ever seen this youth or heard of him again.

As soon as the youth left, the girl came out of her coma, and the next morning made a big fuss because she wanted to go to school. This happened thirty years before the inquest. Meanwhile, the girl has grown up and is still in excellent health.[5]

Another typical case is that of a girl of 12 who was living among people who held frequent spiritualist sessions. She was often afraid of what was going on in the house and frequently prayed for help. One day, as she was walking alone through a woods, she suddenly saw

---

[5]H. C. Moolenburgh, *A Handbook of Angels*, p. 25.

a man in front of her who had not come from anywhere—but just appeared. He was completely ordinary-looking, and came up to her and told her not to be afraid—and from that moment she was not. He also told her that her life would not be easy, but that the Lord would be with her always. The man then disappeared in the same way as he had come.

This meeting left her with a feeling of happiness that lasted for a whole week. From then on, the girl was able to tell whether the spirits that appeared in her house were genuine or not.

Lastly, here is the story of a rescue on the grand scale, that of no less than the whole Finnish army. It has nothing to do with Dr. Moolenburgh's search, but it was he, again, who reported it. In 1939, the powerful Red Army invaded Finland and everyone was convinced that the small Finnish army would soon be annihilated. But no! It succeeded in getting away. As Sir Winston Churchill wrote in his *Memoirs*, this aroused surprise and emotion all round the world. The Russians had mounted a pincer movement, and the Finnish army got out of it, but no one knows how. Their army seems to have become invisible. Years later a member of this army said that, in those dramatic moments "something" was seen—and that something was an angel, who must have worked the miracle.

•   •   •

In concluding his search, Dr. Moolenburgh remarks that if 31 of the 400 people he interviewed say that they have seen an angel, this means that the equivalent number for the entire population of Holland would be remarkable. If one Dutchman in a hundred has seen an angel in a population of 15 million, as many as 150,000 angels would have been seen. This would be the best kept secret of the century!

Moolenburgh believes that he draws angel-types to him because he had an encounter with an angel. In any case, although before beginning his search, Dr. Moolenburgh believed that people used to see angels but no longer see them today; his conclusion after the search is that angels are still seen but most people don't talk about them anymore.

It is to be hoped that the fact of having read about angelic experiences like those reported in this book will induce more people to talk about them. I personally remember that when, about a dozen years ago, I began to collect information for research on what are known as "near-death experiences" I encountered a certain amount of difficulty at first. People were afraid of talking about such ineffable moments. They were scared they would not be believed, or taken for mad; this because they could read the disbelief in the eyes of the first people they shared the experience with. More than one person said to me: "I know you will believe me, and so I willingly tell you what happened to me on the threshold of death. No one has believed me yet, and so I have stopped talking about it."

In just these few years things have changed a great deal. Many books have been published on such experiences, and people worthy of the greatest respect — doctors, psychologists, and university professors — have dealt with the subject. Nowadays, anyone who relates that he or she has been in a coma and seen and heard strange and extraordinary things in that state, is no longer listened to with disbelief, but with interest and participation.

The same thing could well happen, in time, with angels. After all, thinking it over, we are well disposed to talk about devils, organize conventions and meetings to discuss them, read books that speak of them which are more and more often published. So, why should we not believe in the much more comforting and happier presence of "protectors"? To believe in angels can only be positive for us. To turn to them is, in the last analysis, only to appeal to the best part of ourselves and listen to what that soft, but steady and ever-present voice that always urges us to do good has to say. It bids us go out and meet what life has in store, with trust and love, and to raise our eyes on high.

I believe that if we knew how to abandon ourselves to these voices, things would improve—for us, our neighbors and for the world around us. Why don't we give it a try?

Chapter 12

St. Thomas Aquinas
and the Guardian Angels

In the chapter called Beings of Light, we mentioned that Dr. Elisabeth Kübler-Ross, the great American doctor who works with people who are dying, says that all people are accompanied from birth to death by spiritual beings. All people have these escorts, whether we believe it or not. Our own personal beliefs are of no importance, because love is unconditional and everyone receives this gift at birth. To children, these playmates are unseen friends. Dr. Kübler-Ross made this claim on the basis of her years and years of experience at the bedside of people on the point of death. When people are dying, on reaching the "threshold," they meet these friends again, recognize them, and abandon themselves to them trustingly. Dr. Kübler-Ross recorded many of these experiences.

Belief in guardian angels is also a part of religious tradition and teaching. The first reference to the figure of a protector is to be found in Psalm 91: "Because thou hast made the LORD, which is my refuge, even the most High, thy habitation; There shall no evil befall thee, neither shall any plague come nigh thy dwelling. For he shall give his angels charge over thee, to keep thee in all thy ways. They shall bear thee up in their hands, lest thou dash thy foot against a stone" (Psalm 91:9–13).

The doctrine of guardian angels was repeated and codified by *St. Thomas Aquinas* (1226–1274), the great scholar, philosopher, and master theologian, and author of many works. The most important of these is his *Summa Theologiæ*, in which he paid detailed attention to angels and all the theological questions concerning them. His analysis was so shrewd and penetrating, and he was able to express himself so clearly and convincingly that his contemporaries called him Doctor Angelicus.

St. Thomas maintains that the angels are purely immaterial and spiritual, their number is incalculable, and they are divided into hierarchies that differ in degree of wisdom and perfection: Cherubim and Thrones (the 1st hierarchy); Dominations, Virtues and Powers (the 2nd hierarchy); and Principalities, Archangels and Angels (the 3rd hierarchy).

The angels have not always existed, but were created by God, perhaps before the material world and humans were created. They possess the gift of free will—and it is precisely because of this that some of them fell into the sin of pride, arrogance, and envy, becoming fallen angels, Devils incapable of loving God or the human beings He created.

All people—Christian or not—have guardian angels who never leave, even if they become the worst of sinners, according to St. Thomas Aquinas. Guardian angels do not prevent people from making use of their freedom even if they do so for evil purposes. They work to enlighten people and inspire good sentiments. The Devil, for his part, acts on people in the opposite way. If people—perhaps with the help of guardian angels, succeed in overcoming the temptations of the Devil, they earn merit and procure good for themselves. Thus the Devil becomes indirectly God's collaborator in the salvation of human beings.

People can talk to angels, but they do not know the secrets of their hearts (which are known only to God). By doing so they enlighten themselves as to their needs, hopes and desires. This is in synthesis, reduced to the maximum simplicity, the doctrine of angels of Doctor Angelicus.

•　　•　　•

When we turn our thoughts to guardian angels, we generally imagine them in the company of children—and, indeed, it was from a small girl that I got this unusual and special witness.

The girl's name is Giorgia D. She is 8 years old and lives at Pavullo, a small town in the Appenines in the Province of Modena. Her mother is a schoolteacher and her father a doctor. She has a twin sister called Giulia, and a slightly elder brother.

Giorgia is a good-looking girl, intelligent and obedient, very lively and always on the go; one of those who gives the impression that they must have most attentive guardian angels! And, in fact, her life has already been saved on more than one occasion in ways that seem inexplicable, verging on the miraculous. Once she was almost run over by a car, which just managed to pull up when only an inch away from her. Another time, when she was 3, she fell down a mountain precipice: "She landed on her feet and without a scratch after falling I don't know how far," her father remembers. "She seems to have flown!"

Before she was 3, Giorgia began to say that she had a *friend*—and this friend has been with her ever since.

"She talks to her, and talks sense!" says her mother. "She never contradicts herself. Not long ago she went to confession for the first time, and told the priest about him, too. The priest was able to understand—just as we had in the family—that these 'meetings' bring Giorgia a lot of joy and serenity. She doesn't boast about it, but doesn't try to keep it secret, either. It's quite natural to her."

Giorgia talked to me, too, about her special friend. This is how the conversation went:

"So many times! I've heard his voice so many times, even when I was very small!"

"What's this voice like?"

"It's a man's voice, like Daddy's."

"What sort of things does it tell you?"

"Once I fought with a classmate I didn't like. I kicked him and he kicked me back. Then I heard my friend's voice telling me not to kick him again."

"Do you hear the voice only after you've quarrelled?"

"No, also when I haven't. I hear it when I go to bed and think about what happens at school, things that upset me. And my friend tells me not to worry, and to study. He tells me not to be afraid, everything'll be all right!"

"Does your friend come only when he wants to, or do you sometimes call him?"

"Sometimes I call him: I close my eyes and *pull him down with my hands.*[1] Then he comes at once."

"Do you only hear your friend, or see him, too?"

"I usually hear him, but I see him, too, sometimes. The first time was when I was quarrelling with Giulia. He came and told me not to. So I stopped."

---

[1] Giorgia was unable to give any explanation for a gesture that seemed to her instinctive and quite natural.

"What does your friend look like?"

"He wears a long blue dress down to his feet, is fair-haired with greenish-blue eyes. His big, white wings are open. There is light round his head, and some round his body, too. He's taller than I am and always happy. He comes suddenly, then disappears, but I continue to hear his voice."

"Do you see and hear him when other people are with you?"

"Yes, even with others there. At playtime, at school, when I don't know what to do I call him and we talk, we tell each other things . . ."

"Does your sister see him?"

"No, she neither sees nor hears him. When I tell her he's with me, she's afraid!"

"Has he been recently?"

"A few days ago I was quarrelling with Giulia, and he told me to stop it, and so show I was better than she is!"

"Who have you told about your friend?"

"Daddy, Mummy, and the priest, and now you."

"How many times have you seen him, in all?"

"Three times. The last time was in May, when I took, my first communion. I was sitting in the church and he appeared between me and the priest. He looked pleased."

"Did he tell you why he was pleased?"

"He said he was pleased because I was taking communion."

Figure 9. Blowing the Second Trumpet, Dublin Apocalypse. Trinity College, 14th century.

Chapter 13

The Angel
Motif in Art

A ngels have always stimulated the imagination of artists, particularly painters and sculptors. Winged beings and celestial messengers are to be seen in the figurative arts of the Sumerians, Babylonians, Egyptians, Greeks, and Romans. The very famous *Nike* (Victory) of Samothrace, now in the Louvre in Paris, was sculpted in the second century B.C. and is one of the most wonderful winged figures we have and, although female, is very like the angels of the Christian church.

Coming to our own day, we find countless representations of angels in paint, stone, and wood. The favorite scenes are those from the Old Testament, and even more, the New: the Annunciation, the glad tidings to the shepherds, Joseph's dream, the angel on the Mount of Olives, the Ascension, Peter's release from jail and many more. Not to mention the hosts of angel musicians, guardian angels, choirs of angels, and angels bearing candelabra to be found in our churches.

It would take far too long to refer in detail to all this, so I leave it to the illustrations in this book to provide some fine examples of figurative art dedicated to angels. I should, however, like to say something about two of these artists, Hieronymus Bosch and Marc Chagall.

The great Dutch painter Hieronymous Bosch (1450–1516) drew his inspiration from various subjects ranging from magic, the occult, religion and fairy tales. His famous *Ascent to the Empyrean,* which is illustrated on page 105 is the most faithful and impressive representation of what dying people see. We spoke of this in chapter 7 on Beings of Light. And here, again, is the dark tunnel leading to a blinding light, with souls going along it being escorted by their guardian angels.

In Bosch's day, no one spoke of what we call near-death experiences. They have become known only very recently. So, what can have been Bosch's inspiration? It must surely have been a personal experience (which we do not know about) or else one that somebody told him about. What is certain is that Bosch *knew.* And, in the light of what we know today, his painting—which was long considered an allegory or a utopian dream—seems all the more convincing and real.

The second work I wish to mention is that of Marc Chagall, the extraordinary Russian painter who was born in 1887 and died only a few years ago. He lived in Paris and devoted a great deal of his art to the metaphysical, the supernatural, dreams, and symbols. His skies are often inhabited by angels, together with pairs of lovers and fantastic animals in strange colors. And these are not figures of his imagination, but originated in a dream he himself described at some point in his life.

"In those rooms, with workers and pedlars for neighbors, all I had to do was lie down on my bed and mull my life over. And what else could I have thought about? I had dreams: an empty quadrangular room. A bed in one corner with me on it. It is getting dark.

"Suddenly the ceiling of the room opens and a splendid winged figure comes down and fills the room with waves of perfume. Its wings rustle as it moves them.

"An angel! I think. I can't open my eyes, there's too much light, it's blinding!

"The angel hovers in each corner of the room, and then rises up again and disappears through the ceiling, taking all its light with it, and the blue of the sky.

"It is dark again. And I wake up . . ."

We do not know if the angels painted or sculpted by other artists originated—as was probably the case with the two painters we have just discussed—from personal experiences. Perhaps not. They may well be only artistic representations of a theme that stimulates the imagination of all sensitive people. But these two examples from Bosch and Chagall are enough to allow us to consider with different eyes all the representations of angels in the figurative arts.

• • •

A special word needs to be said about William Blake (1757–1827), who lived his life in London and was a poet, painter, and engraver. He illustrated his own books of poetry, which were inspired by a mysticism of a Christian origin.

From his childhood, Blake had visions of spirits and angels. He even claims that an angel taught him how to paint. Apparitions of a supernatural kind came to him throughout his life and appear in his works. He says, for example, that he saw Jesus Christ almost daily, and Jesus Christ dictated what Blake should write. In his poem *Jerusalem*, he wrote that he was only the scribe and that the real authors were in the beyond.

Blake claimed that his drawings, too, were only copies of images that appeared to him and inspired him. He lived his life between two worlds, assured of the reality of both, and succeeded in amalgamating them in his works, thanks to his exceptional personality. For him the best sources of knowledge were intuition and imagination. The angelic and infernal worlds seemed to him to be absolute realities, to be described and reproduced as the things and people of this world. Here is just one example of a "memorable fancy" from his poem *The Marriage of Heaven and Hell*:

> The ancient tradition that the world will be consumed in fire at the end of six thousand years is true, as I have heard from Hell.
>
> For the cherub with his flaming sword is hereby commanded to leave his guard at tree of life; and when he does, the whole creation will be consumed and appear infinite and holy, whereas it now appears finite and corrupt.[2]

•   •   •

Blake was both a painter and a man of letters. When we go on to the theme of angels in literature, itself, there are a multitude of stimulating examples—some more famous than others. Here are one or two.

On the subject of angels in literature, where else should we begin than with the 28th Canto of Dante Alighieri's *Paradise*? It is, in fact, an ideal poetic rendering of the doctrine of Dionysius the Areopagite on the

---

[2]June Singer, *The Unholy Bible: A Psychological Interpretation of William Blake*, "The Marriage of Heaven and Hell," Plate 14 (New York: C. G. Jung Foundation, 1970), p. 124.

angelic hierarchies. Undoubtedly it was the product of the culture of Dante's time, but perhaps also the result of visions and personal experience. It is Beatrice who acts as his guide in Paradise and explains to him about these hierarchies. The extract is from lines 94 to 139:

> I heard Hosannah sung from choir to choir to the fixed point that holds them, and will forever hold them at the *Ubi* in which they have ever been. And she, who saw the questioning thoughts within my mind, said, "The first circles have shown to you the Seraphim and the Cherubim. Thus swiftly they follow their bonds, in order to liken themselves to the point as most they can, and they can in proportion as they are exalted in vision. Those other loves who go round them are called Thrones of the divine aspect, because they terminated the first triad. And you should know that all have delight in the measure of the depth to which their sight penetrates the Truth in which every intellect finds rest; from which it may be seen that the state of blessedness is founded on the act of vision, not on that which loves, which follows after; and the merit, to which grace and good will give birth, is the measure of their vision; thus, from grade to grade the progression goes.
>
> The next triad that thus flowers in this eternal spring which nightly Aries does not despoil perpetually sings Hosannah with three melodies which sound in the three orders of bliss that form the triad. In this hierarchy are the next divinities, first Dominions, then Virtues;

and the third are Powers. Then in the two penultimate dances, the Principalities and Archangels circle; the last is wholly of Angelic sports. These orders all gaze upward and prevail downward, so that toward God all are drawn, and all do draw. And Dionysius with such great desire set himself to contemplate these orders that he named and distinguished them, as I: but Gregory afterward differed from him, wherefore, as soon as he opened his eyes in this heaven, he smiled at himself. And if a mortal declared on earth so much of secret truth, I would not have you wonder, for he who saw it here on high disclosed it to him, with much else of the truth about these circles.[3]

Just the briefest of commentaries: Dante (in line 94) hears the angels singing hosannas to God (the *fixed point*) round which they move incessantly, permeated by his grace. And Beatrice (*she* in line 97) feels intuitively his desire to know the exact order of the angelic hierarchies, the subject of bitter discussion among theologians and wise men (*my inward meditations*), and gives him the explanations he needs. She then speaks of the Seraphim and Cherubim who swiftly follow the ties (*hoops*) of love that link them with God (100); and goes on to speak of the third hierarchy that of the Thrones (104). All three orders of intelligences enjoy a beatitude which is in proportion to the profundity and intensity of their vision of God (106–108). The celestial beatitude (110) depends on being able to see God, and not on love in itself, which descends from the vision.

---

[3]From Dante Alighieri, *The Divine Comedy: Paradiso*, Bollingen Series LXXX (Princeton, NJ: Princeton University Press, 1975), pp. 319, 321.

Beatrice goes on to describe the next three orders (*the other trine*, 115): Dominations, Virtues and Powers, which hymn God in perpetuity. The last two circling gladly (*with glad round*, 124) consist of Principalities (*princedoms*) and Archangels, and the last (*the band angelical Disporting*, 125–6) of festive angels.

These celestial orders (127) concentrate ecstatically on the point where God is, exercising their beneficent influence on the things below them. The description of Diognes (*Dionysius*) (130), the Areopagite, who knew the celestial hierarchies better than anyone else is the one Dante uses.

The reference to Pope, and later Saint, Gregory, is to a theological dispute: Gregory, Dante reminds us, did not accept the doctrine of Diogenes, but was obliged to change his mind once he reached paradise.

•   •   •

Angels (or rather, in this case, archangels) play an important part in the "Prologue in Heaven" to Goethe's *Faust*, the first verses of which we quote. In this prologue to the actual play itself, God and Mephistophiles meet, argue, and wager on Faust's soul. Their dialogue is commented on by the archangels Raphael, Gabriel and Michael:

RAPHAEL:
    The sun sings as it sang of old
    With brother spheres in rival sound,
    In thundrous motion onward rolled
    Completing its appointed round.
    The angels draw strength from the sight,
    Though fathom it no angel may:
    The great works of surpassing might
    Are grand as on Creation day.

GABRIEL:
  And swift beyond conception flies
  The turning earth, now dark, now bright,
  With clarity of paradise
  Succeeding deep and dreadful night;
  The sea in foam from its broad source
  Against the base of cliffs is hurled,
  And down the sphere's eternal course
  Both cliff and sea are onward whirled.

MICHAEL:
  And storms a roaring battle wage
  From sea to land, from land to sea,
  And forge a chain amid their rage,
  A chain of utmost potency.
  There blazing lightning-flashes sear
  The path for bursting thunder's way —
  And yet thy heralds, Lord, revere
  The mild procession of thy day.

ALL THREE:
  The angels draw strength from the sight,
  Though fathom it no angel may;
  The great works of surpassing might
  Are grand as on Creation day.[4]

Goethe, the greatest German poet, was a man of rare sensitivity, and his life was full of particular events linked to the world of the mystic and occult. We cannot, therefore, exclude that he may be speaking from personal angelic experience. The three archangels in this Prologue are, however, more correctly poetical personi-

---

[4]Johann Wolfgang von Goethe, *Faust*, translated with introduction and notes by Charles E. Passage (New York: Bobbs-Merrill, 1965), pp. 12, 13.

fications than messengers of God like those we read
about in the Bible.

• • •

Another great German poet who wrote about
angels is Rainer Maria Rilke. In his *Duinesian Elegies*,
and especially the first and second of them, he devotes
some most beautiful lines to these celestial creatures.
For him they represent to all intents and purposes
what, for Nietzsche's Superman, was the power to
excel oneself, the loftiest and most sublime expression
of beings who become able to ascend to God. To some
critics, Rilke's concept is the most important and
famous of all those elaborated in the whole of
literature—as distinct from those in the religious texts.

"Who are you?" the poet asks of the angels who
appear to him to be "terrible." And they reply:

> Successful first creatures, favorites of creation,
> high mountain ranges, dawn-reddened peaks
> of all creation, pollen of the flowering
>   Godhead,
> junctures of light, avenues, stairways, thrones,
> spaces of essence, shields of ecstasy, storms
> of tumultuously enraptured emotion and
>   suddenly, singly,
> *mirrors* which reconcentrate once again in their
> countenances their own outflowing beauty.[5]

Rilke himself, in a letter of 1925, explained that his
angels had "nothing to do with the angels of the Chris-

---

[5]Ranier Maria Rilke, *Duinesian Elegies*, tr. Elaine E. Boney (Chapel Hill, NC:
University of North Carolina Press, 1975), p. 9.

tian heaven," but were rather much closer to those of Islam.

•   •   •

The theme of angels returns in the final pages of Thomas Mann's famous short story "Death in Venice," which was published in 1912. The plot is well known: Gustav von Aschenbach, a Northern writer and man of culture, comes to spend a holiday in Venice, but there is an outbreak of cholera in the city, which the authorities hush up so as not to frighten off the tourists. Aschenbach remains, and so does the family of the young Tadzio, an exceptionally beautiful Polish adolescent, of whom the writer has become enamored without realizing it. This is the story of that discovery, in the climate of decadence that preceded the First World War and the collapse of 19th-century values.

His death is the sublimation of Aschenbach's life. It takes place on the beach where—as he had done so often—he is watching Tadzio. The youth has just wrestled with a stronger companion, and almost been choked. But he breaks free and walks toward the sea. This is the final scene, in which the youth, in the eyes of the dying writer, becomes an angel of death come to escort him into infinite space:

> He [Tadzio] lingered on the edge of the water with his head down, drawing figures in the wet sand with one toe; then he went into the shallows, which did not cover his knees in the deepest place, crossed them leisurely, and arrived at the sandbank. He stood there a moment, his face turned to the open sea; soon after, he began stepping slowly to the left along

the narrow stretch of exposed ground. Separated from the mainland by the expanse of water, separated from his companions by a proud moodiness, he moved along, a strongly isolated and unrelated figure with fluttering hair—placed out there in the sea, the wind, against the vague mists. He stopped once more to look around. And suddenly, as though at some recollection, some impulse, with one hand on his hip he turned the upper part of his body in a beautiful twist which began from the base—and he looked over his shoulder toward the shore. The watcher sat there, as he had sat once before when for the first time these twilight-gray eyes had turned at the doorway and met his own. His head, against the back of the chair, had slowly followed the movements of the boy walking yonder. Now, simultaneously with this glance, it rose and sank on his breast, so that his eyes looked out from underneath, while his face took on the loose, inwardly relaxed expression of deep sleep. But it seemed to him as though the pale and lovely lure out there were smiling to him, nodding to him; as though, removing his hand from his hip, he were signaling to come out, were vaguely guiding toward egregious promises. And, as often before, he stood up to follow him.[6]

Very shortly afterward (in 1914) we find in *The Diaries of Franz Kafka* a radiant and extraordinary page

---

[6]Thomas Mann, *Death in Venice*, tr. Kenneth Burke (New York: Borzoi, Alfred Knopf, 1965), pp. 111, 112.

devoted to the appearance of an angel. It is not all that different from what we read by Marc Chagall, and is perhaps rather unexpected in Kafka, a man who lived a life of anguish and loneliness, feeling himself a prisoner in his rented room, which was hardly the place for golden dreams. Yet it was just to him that the following experience occurred:

> I paced up and down my room from early morning until twilight. . . . Towards evening I walked over to the window. . . . I happened calmly to glance into the interior of the room and at the ceiling. And finally, . . . this room . . . began to stir. The tremor began at the edges of the thinly plastered white ceiling. Little pieces of plaster broke off with a distinct thud. . . . I held out my hand and some plaster fell into it too. . . . The cracks in the ceiling made no pattern yet, but it was already possible somehow to imagine one. Wave after wave of the colour — or was it light? — spread out towards the now darkening edges. One no longer paid any attention to the plaster that was falling away. . . . Yellow and golden-yellow colours now penetrated the violet from the side. But the ceiling did not really take on these different hues; the colours merely made it somewhat transparent; things striving to break through it seemed to be hovering above it, already one could almost see the outlines of a movement there, an arm was thrust out, a silver sword swung to and fro. . . a vision intended for my liberation was being prepared.
>
> I sprang up on the table . . . tore out the electric light . . . and hurled it to the floor. . . . I

had barely finished when the ceiling did in fact break open. . . . an angel in bluish-violet robes girt with gold cords sank slowly down on great white silken-shining wings, the sword in its raised arm thrust out horizontally. 'An angel, then!' I thought; 'it has been flying towards me all the day and in my disbelief I did not know it. Now it will speak to me.' I lowered my eyes. When I raised them again the angel was still there . . . hanging rather far off under the ceiling (which had closed again), but it was no living angel. . . .

The hilt of the sword was made . . . to hold candles. . . . I had pulled the electric light down . . . there was still one candle left, so I . . . stuck the candle into the hilt of the sword, lit it, and then sat late into the night under the angel's faint flame."[7]

Franz Kafka has left no comment on this extraordinary vision of his, and so we can only try to guess: was it a real encounter? Or did the ceiling open symbolically for a moment to this anguished man, and then close again? If so, it left a tangible sign of its presence in the painted figurehead, which is not a living angel but represents one. What is certain is that Kafka experienced a moment of grace, was given a "sign" that helped and consoled him.

Another thing that seems to me very important is the reference to the fact that a person needs to be doubly disposed for such an *encounter* to take place. The angel had set off to reach the poet, and while in flight

[7]*The Diaries of Franz Kafka 1914–1923*, translated from German by Martin Greenberg. (London: Secher and Warburg, 1949; London: Minerva, 1992), pp. 290–292.

sent him messages which for a long time he failed to pick up. He finally understands, accepts the incredible, prepares himself and makes arrangements for the extraordinary event. Only then does it actually take place. The meaning is clear: only when he is in the right frame of mind and inwardly ready to accept it can anyone pick up such a celestial sign. Until then he is unworthy of a supernatural visitation.

The meeting with the blue and gold angel, descending into the poet's grey room with its great white, rustling wings, is a splendid image, like a rainbow over Kafka's gloomy world. For the poet who better than any other—and in almost prophetic tones—has described the crisis of contemporary man, there was now not only alienation and failure to communicate, but also a celestial sign. One only, as far as we know, but sufficient to enlighten his life, even if with only a candle's faint flame.

•   •   •

Not even Pier Paolo Pasolini was able to duck the fascination of an angel. This peeps out from time to time in the pages of *Teorema* (1968) in the garb of Angelo ("little angel") the postman, who arrives ostensibly to make the afternoon delivery of junk mail (printed matter and unsealed envelopes containing stuff that no one reads), but really to radiate joy and serenity with his presence and echo distant worlds.

The little angel makes his first appearance in the big garden in which Lucia and Odette, the hostesses, are entertaining a guest: "They don't speak, other than to exchange banalities that mean something different, something obscure and perhaps inexpressible . . . ," is how Pasolini describes being together in this way.

And then, unexpectedly, the postman arrives with the curls, neither innocent nor cheeky, as if sent miraculously from the distant city. He brings his useless mail that nobody expects and nobody opens and his laughing eyes communicate fear and simple happiness. Then the little angel goes off singing.

The second appearance of Angelo, the postman, to the protagonists of the novel is even more explicit. They are again shut into a simple, wild, and inexpressive silence, oppressed by something greater than they are. And he arrives as if nothing had happened, with that gaiety of his that comes from other worlds, other peoples. As if miraculously, the others begin to speak. The postman with the curls learns that a problem exists and he becomes their confidant. Certain initiatives are taken, and when things appear to be going really well, and the problem is happily solved, the little Angel leaves—forgetful of everything, disappearing again toward other places, other people, and the other worlds from which he was sent.[8]

A messenger of peace, joy and serenity—the part, indeed, that is traditionally played by angels.

•   •   •

We find ample and surprising references to the angelic hierarchies (although we could equally well have quoted from Friederich Holderlin, Anatole France, Stefan George, Paul Valery, Georg Trakl, Alfred Döblin, or others) in the American writer of Russian origin who earned the Nobel Prize for Literature, Saul Bellow's *Humboldt's Gift* which won him the Pulitzer

---

[8]Pier Paolo Pasolini, *Teorema* (Milan, Italy: Garzanti Ed., 1968).

Prize in 1976.[9] His book is a vast fresco of modern American society, in which the theme of angels provides a sharp contrast. But Bellow clearly suffers from neither remorse nor taboos. Well versed in the writings of Rudolf Steiner, the founder of anthroposophy, he must certainly have been familiar with his doctrines on the superior worlds, and does not shirk producing profound dissertations on Cherubim, Seraphim, and the other angelic orders as quoted by the apostle Paul in his Epistles, a subject he found highly suitable for including in everyday conversations.

The character who discusses angels is Dr. Scheldt, a follower of Steiner and, to some extent, the guru of Citrine, the hero of the novel.

> Then Dr. Scheldt begins to speak on the text, *I am the light of the world*. To him that light is understood also as the sun itself. Then he speaks of the gospel of Saint John as drawing upon the wisdom-filled Cherubim, while the gospel of Saint Luke draws upon the fiery love the Seraphim—Cherubim, Seraphim, and Thrones being the three highest spiritual hierarchy. I am not at all certain that I am following. "I have no experience of any of this advanced stuff, Dr. Scheldt, but I still find it peculiarly good and comforting to hear it all said.[10]

Later, during another conversation, Dr. Scheldt goes deeper into the matter. He says to Citrine:

---

[9]Saul Bellow, *Humboldt's Gift* (New York: Viking Press, 1973).
[10]Saul Bellow, *Humboldt's Gift* (New York: Viking Press, 1973), p. 262.

I questioned him about the Spirits of Form, the Exousiai, known in Jewish antiquity by another name. These shapers of destiny should long ago have surrendered their functions and powers to the Archai, the Spirits of Personality who stand one rank closer to man in the universal hierarchy. But a number of dissident Exousiai, playing a backward role in world history, had for centuries refused to let the Archai take over. They obstructed the development of a modern sort of consciousness. Refractory Exousiai belonging to an earlier phase of human evolution were responsible for tribalism and the persistence of peasant or folk consciousness, hatred of the West and of the New, they nourished atavistic attitudes. I wondered whether this might not explain how Russia in 1917 had put on a revolutionary mask to disguise reaction; and whether the struggle between these same forces might not lie behind Hitler's rise to power as well.[11]

And again:

Certain spiritual beings must achieve their development through men, and we betray and abandon them by this absenteeism. . . . Our duty . . . is to collaborate with the Angels. . . . Guided by the Spirits of Form, Angels sow seeds of the future in us. They inculcate certain pictures into us of which we are "normally" unaware. Among other things they wish to make us see the concealed divinity of other human beings. They show man how he can

---

[11]Saul Bellow, *Humboldt's Gift*, p. 292.

cross by means of thought the abyss that separates him from Spirit. To the soul they offer freedom and to the body they offer love.[12]

The doctrines Saul Bellow refers to are, as we have said, those of Rudolf Steiner, where all human activity is guided by angelic hierarchies that influence us to a greater or lesser effect. And it was hardly to be expected that we should find, in a very modern novel that denounces the alienation of American society, that the angelic hierarchies and their activities are quoted on more than one occasion!

• • •

In the opening chapter, entitled "Gibreel's (i.e., Gabriel's) Angel" of the *Satanic Verses*—a novel by the Anglo-Indian writer Salman Rushdie which came out at the beginning of 1989 and immediately caused an international scandal because of the violent reaction of the Ayatolla Khomeini that led to the book being banned in all Islamic countries—he speaks of the "last temptation of Mahomet."

The novel begins spectacularly: at dawn on an icy winter morning an Air India Jumbo explodes while in flight at six thousand meters above the English Channel. From the tremendous disintegration of people and things there emerge intact only two figures: the famous Indian actor Gibreel Farisha, and another Indian called Saladin Chamcha, a radio personage famous for being able to produce on the air a host of different voices. The two fly through the air for a long time. Saladin, immaculate as ever, has not lost even his bowler hat. But

---

[12]Saul Bellow, *Humboldt's Gift*, pp. 293, 294.

Gibreel is agitated and unable to control his own movements. Both sing and shout, exchange quips and hurl challenges at each other. Finally, as they are flying through a thick, cold cloud curtain, they seek each other and fall to earth embraced, landing miraculously alive on a snow-covered English beach.

The miracle, however, brings about a radical change in each of our heroes. Gibreel turns into a sort of modern Archangel with a pale golden light emanating from his whole body. Saladin realizes with consternation that horns are sprouting on his forehead, his thighs are becoming horny and hairy, and he has cloven hooves instead of feet.

Having thus become the symbols of good and evil, Gibreel and Saladin continue to live in the world and witness a sparkling series of fantastic and symbolical adventures, in which Good and Evil are indissolubly linked, and the destinies of the angel Gibreel and the devil Saladin interwoven.[13]

•   •   •

These few examples have been chosen from many possibilities to show how the subject of angels is treated in art. The examples demonstrate how far and with what intensity the figures of celestial messengers have been present at all times in our history, culture, and imagination. Angels are a symbol of joy and hope, an archetype (to use Dr. Jung's terminology) deeply rooted in the human psyche—still today apparently untouched by the secularization of religion and the oblivion into which our myths have fallen.

---

[13]Salman Rushdie, *Satanic Verses* (New York and London: Viking Penguin, 1989).

Figure 10. The alchemist meets an angelic guide. Woodcut from the Musaeum Hermeticum Reformatum et Amplicatum, 17th century.

Chapter 14

Two Interviews about Angels

To my treatise on angels I now add two interviews with our celestial protectors. They are both personal "angelic experiences" actually lived by the persons concerned. I am extremely grateful to both for their willingness, through this book, to share with others what was granted them. The first is with Signora Giuliana of Rome, a charismatic; the second with Father Eugenio Ferrarotti of Genoa.

By "charisma" we mean a particular gift from above conveying the power to convince doubters. Traditionally, charisma came as the gift of clairvoyance, speaking in tongues, the laying on of hands, and writings. There is mention of these abilities in the Acts of the Apostles. The phenomenon seems to be returning today, perhaps because the Third Millennium is approaching, which is expected to be that of the spirit.

Signora Giuliana has for twenty years been granted the gift of writing. It came to her after the death of her only son Armando, who was just 20 years old.

"After Armando was taken from us before his time by a relentless illness," she says, "I began to hear his voice speaking to me. I thought it must have been the grief that enabled me to hear someone who was no more, and so to convince me, he told me that he would send me more important personages, and thus I should be able to understand that this was no hallucination of mine. And that was what happened: the greatest Italian poets came to dictate their verses to me, the Fathers of the Church to inspire me with theological writings. Not only was I not at a level to be able to write such things, but I was not even very religious. I was a believer, but had never sought to deepen my faith and was not a regular churchgoer. These writings, and specially the theological ones, have been examined by priests and experts who found them to be of a high standard and in accordance with the traditions of the Fathers. They convinced me that they were not productions of my own, but something that came to me from outside.

"Since then I have always continued to write: as well as the poets and Fathers, my son came, and also dead people who were generally recognized by others; guardian angels came—in particular Armando's, who told me he was called Astralio, and my own, whose name is Clarus. I also received writings that seem to me to have been inspired by the Madonna and by Jesus. I always showed them to priests, and especially to Father Roschini, a Mariologist, and they never found anything that conflicted with the teachings of the Church. Thus I have been able to go serenely on with a clear conscience."

"Let us consider in particular the messages from angels. Did you expect to be in contact with them?"

"I didn't believe that angels could speak, and wasn't even sure they really existed. Then, through the messages that came to me, I understood that angels do exist, because they told me things that only they could have known!"

"How do you pick up these messages?"

"I generally hear voices, but with the angels, things are different: they dash things at my head like waves. They send not words but vibrations. Angels are pure spirit and generally do not speak except on special occasions, as when the archangel Gabriel, who was Mary's guardian angel, went to her, appeared as a person and spoke audibly to her. Generally, though, the contact is telepathic."

"Are you really convinced that they exist?"

"I had to convince myself: I have had so many proofs, so much help also in ordinary everyday things. All they need is our faith and trust in them."

"How do you communicate with angels?"

"Each one of us has an angel, and to communicate with him it is enough to think of him, pray to him, speak to him. He is always in contact with us, and it is our thought that calls him. If we think about him he comes and acts. If, on the other hand, we never think of him, it is more difficult to make contact. An angel needs a connection, which can be made only by our thinking. Once everyone believed in guardian angels, today I fear that not even all those in religious orders believe in them. Yet the Gospel is interspersed with angelic interventions—from the Annunciation to the Resurrection of Jesus."

"What do the angels tell you in their messages?"

"They speak to me about paradise, which they call harmony. They explain how it is that we can meet each other when we leave the earth. They say that time does not exist, that there is no before and no after, just an always. They often repeat that each of us has an angel, even those who seem to be evil."

"How do you explain the fact that some people can be evil if they have an angel at their side?"

"The angel gives good advice, but as well as him we have a devil and are therefore always tempted.[1] Some of us are more receptive to the advice of our angel and some to that of our devil. It depends on many things — our temperament, circumstances, how we were born. But we cannot judge who's bad. Perhaps not even the worst of them is really wicked, even if he seems to be. We should always remember the parable of the talents. The angels respect the freedom of every one of us, they don't influence us directly, but restrict themselves to giving us inspiration, suggesting good thoughts. It's up to us to follow them."

"Do angels speak of the devil?"

"Now and then, but not often; they prefer to speak of the true reality, of what they call harmony."

"On the basis of what the angels have told you, do people in the beyond remain as they are here?"

"Of course, we keep our fundamental features, otherwise how could we recognize each other? We must find our loved ones just as they were when they left us. What sort of a paradise would it be if we couldn't rediscover and recognize each other?"

"Do the angelic hierarchies exist?"

"Yes, just as described in the Scriptures. They were established by God when he created the angels, before the creation of human beings. The angels are always happy because they are already in paradise. They have made their choice and been rewarded. They say that in paradise you never get tired; but they also say that there are no words to describe it. We here on Earth cannot even understand what eternity is. It certainly isn't something slow as it might seem to us, it's a per-

---

[1]Swedenborg, too, speaks of this double presence people have, specifying that it is due to them that we are free to choose good or evil.

manent mode of being. We must have faith in what we shall find when we are in the beyond."

"Have the angels explained to you why we have to live a life here on Earth?"

"Because it is a trial. How could we appreciate the happiness of heaven if we had not experienced the difficulties of life on Earth? Even the sin of Adam and Eve was a good, because if we had always remained in the earthly paradise we should never have understood the beauty of the celestial dimension that is waiting for us after death. Life on Earth is a final and irreversible trial."

"A trial, though, that may appear most unjust: there are such a lot of differences between the lives of one person and another!"

"No, it isn't unjust; the angels have told me that before coming into this world we have a momentary vision of what our life will be and can make a choice. It is we who choose. It is no injustice of God's that some of us are born healthy and others diseased! We are like cells, we pre-exist in God's eternal thought. When we are born, God breathes life into that cell, kindles it: it is in that instant that we see and choose the number of trials we wish to undergo. Then we forget about it completely and live our lives without any recollection of that choice. The cell is an integral part of ourselves, the part that has not been subject to original sin, because it was created before Adam and Eve. Later it will be this integrated cell that constitutes our body in glory, equal to our physical body but better, young and healthy — like the body of Christ and that of the Madonna who were free from original sin. The independent choice of a certain kind of trial depends on the courage of the cell. The angels do not speak of reincarnations."

"Nevertheless, great spirits and men of genius, exceptional people who seem different and better prepared appear to have had previous experiences behind them."

"They are beings like us, only more intelligent. In paradise, happiness is the same for everyone: it's as if we were so many glasses and bottles—each as full as it can contain and that's quite enough for it."

"Is progress possible in the other dimension?"

"Yes, in purgatory, where there is no punishment, just separation from God. As we purify ourselves and evolve there comes to us a complete vision of the Father. And our angel is close to us even in purgatory. Its task is to help us achieve a loftier state."

"The figures of light that certain people, who were on the point of death and were then brought back to life, say they saw beside them, were they really angels?"

"Of course! They're our guardian angels—in some cases it is Christ himself."

"What do you think of the so-called angelic rescues? Some people are convinced they have been rescued by angels."

"I, too, know about some of these cases. In some of them the rescue is made by the guardian angel, others are cases of children who left Earth at a tender age. My son Armando, for example, explained to me that he helps certain people, that he has certain missions, for example to help people avoid certain gestures, such as suicide. It is also possible that they have been seen for an instant—and those who have seen them have always described them as young people. Let me repeat something Father Roschini, the priest who has followed me for so many years, told me. Another priest, a friend of his who was a missionary in Amazonia, was lost in the forest. So he began to pray and call for help. He suddenly heard a voice, raised his eyes and saw a boy who said to him in Italian: 'Father, you're lost. Go in this direction . . .' And he pointed to a certain track. The priest was astonished to have met an Italian in the Amazonian forest. Nevertheless, he looked in the direction he had been shown and tried to remember the instructions exactly. When he looked back toward the boy, he had disappeared. So he followed the track he had been shown and was saved . . ."

"Why do you think you were granted the gift of making these contacts?"

"The Lord moves in so many different ways, and He alone knows why. According to me there aren't any special merits, we who have these contacts are like anyone else; perhaps we are just strategically better-equipped for the purpose. I accepted these facts after a great deal of hesitation, and my husband, too. Today we are pleased, but our name should not be made known. It would be no use; it's the message that matters."[2]

"Why are so many charismatic messages arriving today?"

"Because today there is a great need for them. The Church is a bit lacking, and so God is making use of everyone to increase faith. And perhaps certain things said and written by lay people like myself are more effective. We are not trained to write certain things independently! Lastly, I also believe that God chooses people who are not particularly mystical, who do not live permanently fingering their rosaries! People from whom nobody would have expected anything of the sort, precisely because they cause a bigger stir and are more convincing!"

---

[2]In fact, the various books containing the messages received by Signora Giulia were published anonymously. The one dealing with angelic messages is called *I dettati degli angeli* and can, like the others, be requested from the Libreria Propaganda Mariana, via Acciaioli, 10, 00186, Rome.

"Has this gift of writing and contact with the angels helped you to overcome your grief at the death of your son?"

"Certainly, after Armando's death this charisma helped me and my husband. Yet we still miss our son, we long for him as we have always done. But he has explained that it was his destiny not to stay on Earth very long. So we are looking forward trustingly to meeting him again in heaven!"

•   •   •

Father Eugenio Ferrarotti is a priest of great humanity and experience. It is fifty years since he took his vows, and he lives in the Congregation of the Fathers of San Filippo Neri. He was a Superior in Turin for nearly thirty years, and is now the Superior of the Church of San Filippo in Genoa. He has long been interested in paranormal events because he loves his neighbors and wants to understand, console, and perhaps even guide them on this path—which can be risky if it is taken without enough prudence and balance. Father Eugenio was authorized many years ago by Cardinal Siri to practice exorcism, and this authorization has been renewed by the present Archbishop of Genoa, Monsignor Canestri.

Father Ferrarotti not only observes paranormal phenomena from outside, but also takes part in them. As he himself reveals in this interview, he is able to produce automatic writing—and it is mainly through this means that he has made contact with his guardian angel.

"Father Ferrarotti, is the existence of guardian angels the official teaching of the Church?"

"Of course, it's an element of faith. There are about three hundred mentions of angels in the Scriptures, and Jesus himself speaks of them. Therefore, to remain silent today on the presence of angels amounts to belittling slightly the word of the Lord, censuring it and interpreting it incorrectly. Devotion to our guardian angels should come immediately after that for the Holy Trinity, Jesus, and the Madonna. Guardian angels are a wonderful gift of God. Our souls are, at one and the same time, too great and too fragile to be left alone in this world. The crossing is so delicate and our means so unsure that the Divine Goodness has taken care to provide that we are led from birth to death by an angel who is always at our side: from the moment our soul issues from the creative hands of the Heavenly Father, until after our bodily death. The funeral liturgy reminds us of this: in the benediction at the tombside we pray to God to entrust these mortal remains to the vigilance of the guardian angel! Yes, there are angels all around us; they enlighten us, protect, rule, and defend us on our return journey to the Heavenly Father."

"How can we make contact with our guardian angels?"

"First and foremost by thinking of them. If you don't think about him, yours is as if his hands were tied. But he is able to help and protect you all the same. Who can tell how many times he saves us from spiritual and physical dangers? My St. Philip, for example, was in a very narrow street in Rome one day, with a deep ditch full of slimy water on one side of it. A carriage came along with its four horses out of control and the Saint was lifted up as it were by his hair and thus saved. There's a painting of the event here in our church. So, we need to think of our angels, invoke them and entrust ourselves to them at particularly difficult moments. I do, often, especially when I have to talk to difficult or inaccessible people, or face complicated and intricate problems. I entrust myself to my angel, ask him to go to the angels of the people involved and see about setting things right! It works! This was not my idea, though, but something I was taught by Pope Pius XI, who once confided to Monsignor Roncalli, the future Pope John XXIII, that when he had to meet certain people he set his guardian angel to work and things went better. I advise everyone to try it! And so, an angel needs thinking about, invoking, to have a job to do to keep him busy, because he appears to those who invoke him. Certain Saints felt him beside them, or even saw him close to them in the guise of a handsome youth, sometimes without wings. Or else they felt his presence.[3]

"Do angels always appear as male figures?"

"Generally, yes, the Scriptures present them thus. There are millions, thousands of millions of angels, not just your guardian angel. There's the angel of the day, the angel of your country, the angel of the parish, of the community. Angels have special tasks to perform, to help parish priests do their work well, for example. There are myriads and myriads of them and they form a bridge from us men to God. St. Thomas Aquinas says in his *Summa Theologicæ* that in the space between men and God (he calls it an 'interspace') there are angels who guide people, and it is they who control corporeal things—health, interests, and a bit of everything."

---

[3]Padre Pio, for example, was a great devotee of angels. "May the angel of the Lord be with you and open doors for you," he used to say to those who asked for his blessing. In his book *La verità su angeli e arcangeli*, Giuseppe Del Ton relates that he heard Padre Pio speak the following words: "The angels are so obedient that it seems impossible!" And he suggested to a lady from Turin, Amelia Benedetti: "When you are in need, send me your guardian angel!" Another lady, from Genoa, Ada Sturla, had asked him for spiritual help from a distance and he replied: "Pray to your guardian angel and always send him to me when you are in need."

"*So, we all should think about guardian angels, and can we also give them tasks to perform?*"

"Yes, but have great respect for their presence. This is what the nuns taught us as children, and it was extremely important training for us. If a child treasures it, he acquires a delicacy of conscience that is the real Holy fear of God."

"*Father Ferrarotti, you have had a personal experience with your guardian angel. Would you like to speak about it?*"

"It was something very beautiful that came about of itself. I had been interested in parapsychology for years. A sensitive from Venezuela I met years ago at a congress here in Genoa told me that within six months I should begin to produce automatic writing. I had never thought of any such possibility, and yet, after that meeting, I tried. But I did not succeed until the six months had almost passed. It was just about six months later that I tried again and my hand immediately began to move very rapidly: I wrote in my own handwriting, only slightly altered."

"*How do you produce this automatic writing?*"

"I first cross myself, pray to the Father and create a mental vacuum. When my mind is empty of exterior personal thoughts, my hand begins to move. What surprised me was that at the end there was this signature: 'I am your guardian angel.' I hadn't thought at all about my angel. From then on, though, it has always gone like that. Every time I 'write' the signature is that of my angel."

"*Do you often write?*"

"No, only rarely, when I feel I want to, or am in need of enlightenment. Or else if I want to know whether I behaved well under certain circumstances, or what I can do to help someone. Above all, this contact is a great encouragement to me. I have such serenity inside me and attribute this to a grace for which I must thank God or my angel . . ."

"Are you quite sure it is your angel? Have you ever had any doubts?"

"I have had lots of doubts. Then something happened to me that banished them. Years ago I went to a session of the Florentine medium Roberto Seni. I had met him almost by chance some time before and knew that when in trance he was able to materialize objects, jewels mainly, which he always presented to one of those present. They materialized in his hands, which at that moment shone with a bluish light sufficient to illuminate the whole room. I had gone to Florence with a friend, but did not think I should be allowed into the session because the number of participants had already been reached. I expected to have to follow it through a loudspeaker in the next room. But, as soon as Roberto saw me, he showed me in. Half way through the session, when the materialization had already begun, I heard myself being called by name (no one in that room knew that my name was Eugenio). I approached the medium and he dropped into my hands a small cylindrical mass of bright, incandescent magma. At the same time, he advised me to close my hands and not open them until the session ended. I obeyed. But, from time to time I took a peep and could see that this shining object was changing color slightly and taking shape. I thought to myself that I was extremely lucky. I had not expected to be able to attend the session, but Roberto had not only called me in but presented me with an object that was materializing in my hands! I wondered if it would turn out to be a crucifix or the face of the Madonna . . . At the end of the session I opened my hands and saw a little angel in cast-silver! No such thought had crossed my mind, I hadn't dreamt it might turn out to be an angel! That for me was a confirmation of my automatic writing, and this event also convinced me of the positive aspect of certain spiritualistic sessions, at which only beings of light appear."

"I imagine your devotion to your guardian angel increased from then on?"

"I am always devoted to my guardian angel and my thoughts constantly go to him, and I should like everybody to love this invisible, but intensely real personage. I should never dare to ask to see him, but am quite sure he is close to me. I often think of these fine words in Holy Scripture: 'Behold, I send an angel before thee, to keep thee in the way, and to bring thee into the place which I have prepared. Beware of him and obey his voice' (Exodus 23:20)."

"How do you imagine him?"

"I imagine him clothed, bathed in light. Yes, in the light a representative of the angelic spirit can offer. In fact, my angel often signs himself like this: 'I wrap you in my light which is the divine light . . .' The angels have no corporeal shells—but are eyes that see, ears that hear, hands that touch, and hearts that love. I don't see him, but he sees me, and that is enough for me. Perfect knowledge of the future and the intimate things of the human heart is the prerogative of God alone. An angel knows the future because it is revealed to him by immediate intuition of God's spirit. In any case—from pure, shrewd and extremely subtle conjecture—he knows the secrets of people's hearts: 'The most difficult thing for us is to practice moderation, the wisdom that knows only the limitation of all things!' This was told to me. And this sense of moderation is possessed by the angels and they teach it to us by the example of their careful and solicitous goodness."

"What does your guardian angel communicate to you through your writings?"

"Mainly personal things. That's why I prefer to be alone when I write. I am very pleased to have this possibility of contact with my angel, but I don't overdo it. On the contrary I rarely make use of it."

"Is your contact with your angel always through your writing?"

"No. When I haven't time to write, or don't feel like it, yet need advice on something I am uncertain about, I concentrate and feel an answer inside myself that guides me. Then I feel more confident. Perhaps my confidence at certain moments in helping people who turn to me comes from him, from my angel. But I don't want him to take my place. I want to preserve my own personality, my individuality. His angel, in any case, does not interfere with a person's freedom, he helps but respects personal liberty. As the Holy Fathers say, guardian angels have a mission of peace, penitence, and prayer. Peace in the sense that liberates and prevents disturbances from outside, above all those of the soul. This is a most exacting task. Penitence in the sense that they make us feel remorse. This comes from our conscience, but is also a warning from our guardian angels. Prayer in that they pray for us because they want to save us. I should also like to mention another most important task of guardian angels—that of keeping the devil at bay. Our angel will, in fact, be present at the moment of our death, to frustrate his last deceits. And the archangel Michael will be there, too, whose specific task it is to help dying people. During an exorcism the devil has often said: 'They stole him from me at the last moment!' Who, if not the angels?"

Chapter 15

The Bicameral Mind and the Capacity to Listen to the Gods

Before concluding this anthology of traditions and testimonies on angels, one consideration comes spontaneously to mind. As can be gleaned from so many writings from the past, and in particular the sacred texts and epic poems of all our civilizations, long ago human beings accepted the reality of supernatural beings as natural, and knew how to listen to their voices. We might almost say that there existed a direct channel, a hot line between the inhabitants of earth and the higher spheres.

Today, with a few exceptions, the channel seems to have been blocked and the hot line has snapped. The profound interior unrest of modern people is consequent on this. And so is our—often clumsy and grossly erroneous—search for alternative solutions, and growing nostalgia for the transcendent and the mysterious.

How can we explain this breakdown in relationships? Why is it that we are no longer able to "lend an ear to the gods?" Is there a reason for our deafness toward voices that (as is shown by the evidence presented in this book) are definitely there, ready to speak to us? Is there a reason that we are blind to presences that are nevertheless ready to help us? Recent discoveries in psychology and neurology may be able to give us an answer. Let us consider them.

In his interesting and thoroughly documented book *The Origin of Consciousness in the Breakdown of the Bicameral Mind*,[1] which quite apart from its intrinsic merits has the (fairly rare) advantage of being attractively written and easy to read—Julian Jaynes—an experimental psychologist and Professor at Princeton University, presents a theory of his own that is enlightening also in that it refers to our celestial protectors and therefore seems to me worthy of quotation here.

Julian Jaynes starts from our present-day knowledge of the structure of the human brain. It is by now common knowledge that our two cerebral hemispheres perform different functions: the left controls language, rationality, logic, and our conscious existence. The right is concerned with intuition, imagination, creativity, and emotion. We, today, let ourselves be guided predominantly by the left hemisphere of the brain, and take very little notice of the impulses and stimuli that come from the right. Professor Jaynes goes so far as to call this the "dumb" hemisphere, which makes itself heard only in moments of creativity and on those rare occasions when we succeed in having intuitions, prophetic or clairvoyant flashes, mystical enlightenments or religious experiences.

We do not yet know a great deal about this right hemisphere, and his stimulating theory is that it was once "inhabited" by the gods and ready to listen to their voices. A "bicameral mind," with each hemisphere open and active, is an archaic concept—archaic not so

---

[1] Julian Jaynes, *The Origin of Consciousness in the Breakdown of the Bicameral Mind* (Boston: Houghton Mifflin, 1976).

much in the sense of primitive as of remote in time, antiquated, no longer current.

Our loss of the ability to listen to the gods is said to be compensated for by our conquest of consciousness — a hard-won victory that entailed suffering, but one that has made us what we are today. For good or ill.

Professor Jaynes is an extremely well-read man who has gone deeply into the study of classical history and literature. He provides a long series of examples of literary and archaeological evidence that show how, in antiquity, we were not conscious in the way in which we understand the word today, but let ourselves be guided by the "voices of the gods." He has this to say about Homer's *Iliad*.

> The characters of the *Iliad* do not sit down and think out what to do. They have no conscious minds such as we say we have, and certainly no introspections. It is impossible for us with our subjectivity to appreciate what it was like. When Agamemnon, king of men, robs Achilles of his mistress, it is a god that grasps Achilles by his yellow hair and warns him not to strike Agamemnon (I:197ff.). It is a god who then rises out of the gray sea and consoles him in his tears of wrath on the beach by his black ships, a god who whispers low to Helen to sweep her heart with homesick longing, who hides Paris in a mist in front of the attacking Menelaus, a god who tells Glaucus to take bronze for gold (6:234ff.), a god who leads the armies into battle, who speaks to each soldier at the turning points, who debates and teaches Hector what he must do, who urges the soldiers on or defeats them by casting them in spells or draw-

ing mists over their visual fields. It is the gods who start quarrels among men (4:437ff.), that really cause the war (3:164ff.), and then plan its strategy (2:56ff). It is one god who makes Achilles promise not to go into battle, another who urges him to go, and another who then clothes him in a golden fire reaching up to heaven, and screams through his throat across the bloodied trench at the Trojans, rousing in them ungovernable panic. In fact, the gods take the place of consciousness. . . . The beginnings of action are not in conscious plans, reasons and motives; they are in the actions and speeches of gods.[2]

Scholars have translated the concept of *ka* which is found in Egyptian inscriptions as spirit, ghost, double, vital force, nature, luck, destiny, and what have you. The hieroglyphic symbol for ka is admonishing, for two arms are uplifted and have outspread hands. A man's ka was an articulate voice that he heard inwardly.[3] So, why not as the voice of a divine messenger, a protector or guardian?

There are, Professor Jaynes points out, numerous similar traditions in early civilizations, such as those of Mesopotamia, Israel, Peru and Mexico. With the coming of consciousness, the invention of writing and birth of philosophy, this bicameral mind, which was the source of authority and religious cults, loses its identity and ability to command attention. The archaic world disappears and the modern is born, the last stage in a long process of "a shift from an auditory mind to a

---

[2]Julian Jaynes, *The Origin of Consciousness in the Breakdown of the Bicameral Mind*, p. 72.
[3]Julian Jaynes, *The Origin of Consciousness in the Breakdown of the Bicameral Mind*, p. 190.

visual mind."[4] What we call history, Jaynes says, is only the "slow withdrawing tide of divine voices and presences."[5]

Professor Jaynes also interprets along the same lines the story of the fall of man. He says that this spurious idea of lost innocence that takes its mark in the breakdown of the bicameral mind is the first great conscious narratization of mankind. It is reflected in the Assyrian psalms, the wail of Hebrew hymns, the myth of Eden, the fall from divine favor that is the premise of the world's great religions. This hypothetical fall is due to the groping of newly conscious men to talk about what has happened to them. They have lost the divine voices and assurances in a maze of selfish privacies.

The mind, it is undeniable, has developed more and more unilaterally (the left hemisphere), nevertheless its "bicamerality" has not altogether disappeared, as is shown by the existence of a psyche and flashes from the right hemisphere, that we still experience today. The predominance of the left hemisphere is unable to cancel altogether the other half of the brain.

We are, in fact, filled with nostalgia for this other mind, and certain phenomena we happen to experience constantly remind us of this—the phenomena of telepathy and clairvoyance, prophecies, the perception of voices and presences—and, why not?—sometimes even schizophrenia.

Quoting Shelley who wrote in his *Defence of Poetry*: "The mind in creation is as a fading coal which some invisible influence, like an inconstant wind, awakens to

---

[4]Julian Jaynes, *The Origin of Consciousness in the Breakdown of the Bicameral Mind*, p. 269.
[5]Julian Jaynes, *The Origin of Consciousness in the Breakdown of the Bicameral Mind*, p. 320.

transitory brightness,[6] Jaynes maintains that conscious contemporary man is unable to prophesy the approach or retreat of this revivifying breeze.

Nevertheless—also on the basis of all the experiences gathered in this book—I claim that, with a grain of optimism, we may suggest that the macroscopic development of the left hemisphere may now be compensated and balanced by a revitalization of the right, thanks to which, without renouncing our consciousness and therefore going back to being archaic, we may again begin to hear the voice of the gods and angels.

---

[6]Percy Bysshe Shelley, *Selected Poetry and Prose*, "Defence of Poetry" (New York and London: Routledge English Texts, 1991), lines 927-930.

Chapter 16

An Angelic Fairy Tale

The idea of writing a conclusion to a book that set out to tell some "tales" about angels made me feel slightly embarrassed. Here and there in the course of preparing the text I have—almost without meaning to—made a remark or observation on the value and significance these events may, still today, have on us. But to come to a definite conclusion is quite another matter.

The only thing I really feel like saying is that collecting these angelic adventures has brought me serenity and happiness. I ran into more than one of them almost "by chance," and even got the impression that during the months of preparation material seems to have fallen into my hands without my looking for it. I had never imagined I should have been able to collect so much.

While writing this book, the hours I was able to devote to it were the best hours of my day, and I was sorry when at a certain point I realized that I had finished. Usually it is the other way round: I'm relieved when, at last, the text is ready to be handed to the publisher. This time, though, it was like having, against my will, to say goodbye to a dear friend I have known and loved for as long as I can remember and to whom I have become really close lately. I know that I shall still be able to call on this friend whenever I want to, yet having to stop working in his company saddened me. In other words, I should like to go on writing this book for much longer, simply because of the feelings of joy and harmony its protagonists, the angels, brought me – and that, I hope, they will in turn bring to its readers.

For all these reasons, I have not felt up to writing a proper conclusion, and prefer to leave the matter open and consider this book the first chapter of a long story yet to be written.

While I was working on the last chapter of the book and wondering how I should be able to end it, a kind person I don't know (perhaps a reader of my articles in some magazine) sent me – just like that for no apparent reason – one of Andersen's fairy tales entitled *The Angel* – a lovely story, full of poetry which I now offer my readers instead of a conclusion. Here it is: I find in it something already encountered in the preceding chapters – and think perhaps it is rather more than a fairy tale.

The Angel

Every time a child dies, an angel of the Lord comes down to earth, takes the dead child in his arms, spreads his large white wings and flies to all the places the child had loved. He then picks a posy of flowers and takes them to God, so that they may bloom there even more beautifully than on Earth. The good God takes the flowers to his heart, kisses the one that is dearest of all to him, and this one is granted a voice and allowed to sing in the choir of the blessed.

All this was said by an angel of the Lord as he brought a dead child to heaven, and the child experienced it as a dream; and they flew through the house, to the places where the child had played, and then to the delightful gardens full of very beautiful flowers.

"Which shall we take to plant in heaven?" the angel asked.

In the garden there was a tall rosebush, but a bad man had snapped the stem, and so all the branches heavy with half-open buds had wilted and were dying.

"Poor plant," the child said, "take that one, so that it may bloom close to God."

So the angel picked that plant, and kissed the child, causing him to open his eyes for a moment. They gathered those magnificent flowers, but also picked a derided marigold and a wild violet.

"Now we have the flowers," the child said, and the angel nodded, but they did not yet fly off toward God. It was night and all was silent. They stayed in the big city and flew down one of the narrowest streets, where there was a pile of straw, ashes, and other rubbish; someone had moved house and there were bits of plates and plaster, scraps of cloth and discarded objects strewn everywhere.

The angel pointed to the fragments of a flowerpot on that heap of rubbish. Near them there was a clump of earth that had fallen out of the pot, but remained compact because of the roots of a big wild flower that had withered, was now worthless and so had been thrown away.

"We'll bring it with us," said the angel, "I'll tell you why as we go along." As they flew away the angel told him this story.

Down there in that narrow street, in a basement flat, a poor, sick boy was living. He had been confined to bed ever since he was born. When he felt well enough, he was able to walk about the room on crutches, but that was all he could manage. On certain summer days the sun's rays shone into his room for half an hour, and the little boy sat up to feel the warmth of the sun on his body and watch the red blood run through his thin fingers as he held them up in front of his face. On those days you might have said: 'The little lad went out today!'

All the boy knew about the springtime green of the woods was that a neighbor's son used to bring him a branch of the first beech tree to grow leaves, and he used to put it on his head and dream he was sitting in the sun's rays as it shone, listening to the song of the birds. One spring day the neighbor's son brought him some wild flowers, too, one of which happened still to have its root. And so it was planted in a pot and placed on the windowsill near his bed.

The flower, planted by a loving hand, grew, put out new shoots and flowered every year. It became the boy's wonderful paradise, his little treasure on Earth. He watered it and tended it, seeing that it was put in the last rays of sun that shone through the low window. And the flower grew in the boy's imagination as well, because it was blooming for him, putting out its scent for him and making his life happier. And when the Lord called the boy to himself, he turned toward that flower as he was dying.

For over a year now he has been with God, and for a whole year the flower was left abandoned on the windowsill and has withered. That is why it was thrown on the rubbish heap when the removal took place. And we have included that flower, that poor withered flower, in our posy, because that flower had brought more joy than the more beautiful ones in the real garden.

"But, how do you know all this?" the boy the angel was taking to heaven asked.

"I know because I was that poor sick boy who walked on crutches!" the angel explained. "And I know my own flower very well!"

The child opened its eyes wide and looked at the handsome and happy face of the angel. At that moment they reached heaven, where all was joy and beatitude. God pressed the dead child to His heart, and wings immediately sprang from him, like those of the other angel, and they flew off together hand-in-hand.

Then God pressed the posy to his heart and kissed the poor withered wild flower, and it immediately had a voice and sang with all the angels as they hovered round God; some very near to Him, others far away in the infinite, but all equally happy. And they all sang, large and small, and the good and blessed child sang too, and so did that poor wild flower that had withered and been thrown out into the dark and narrow street, onto the heap of rubbish left after a removal.

Figure 11. At length for hatching ripe, he breaks the shell. William Blake, 1793.

Bibliography

Adler, Gerhard, *Erinnerung an die*. Engel, Herder, 1986.

Alighieri, Dante, *The Divine Comedy: Paradiso*, Bollingen Series LXXX. Princeton, NJ: Princeton University Press, 1975.

Apocrifi dell'Antico Testamento. A cura di Paolo Sacchi Utet, 1981.

Aquinas, St. Thomas, *Summa Theologiæ*. New York and London: McGraw-Hill and Eyre of Spottiswoode, 1968.

Balducci, Corrado, *La Possessione Diabolica*. Rome: Edizioni Mediterranee.

Bellow, Saul, *Humboldt's Gift*. New York: Viking Press, 1973.

Bornaventura da Bagnoregio (San), *Vita di San Francesco d'Assi*. Rome: Edizioni Porziuncola.

Cacciari Massimo, *L'Angelo neccessario*. Milan: Adelphi, 1986.

Chagall, Marc, *My Life*. Chester Springs, PA: Dufour Editions, 1985.

Charles, R. H., *The Book of Enoch*. Oxford: Clarendon Press, 1912.

_____. *The Book of Jubilees* or *The Little Genesis*. London: Society for Promoting Christian Knowledge, 1917.

Coppini, Beatrice, *La scrittura e il percorso mistico. Il 'liber' di Angela da Foligno*. Editrice Ianua, 1986.

Corbin, Henri, *Il paradosso del monoteismo*. Marietti, 1986.

Da Riese, Fernando, *Padre Pio da Pietralcina*. Ed. P. Pio da Pietralcina, 1984.

Del Ton, Giuseppe, *Verità su angeli e arcangeli*. Giardina ed., 1985.

_____. "Il ritorno degli angeli: servitori e custodi," in *Prospettive nel mondo* (Rome, March, 1989): pp. 151, 152.

Dionysius the Areopagite, *The Mystical Theology and The Celestial Hierarchies*. Godalmins, Surrey, UK: The Shrine of Wisdom, 1949.

Eggenstein, Kurt, *The Prophet Jakob Lorber Predicts Coming Catastrophies and the True Christianity*. St. Petersburg, FL: Valkyrie Publishing House, 1979.

Felici, Icilio, *Fatima*. Milan: Ed. Paoline, 1979.

The Findhorn Community, *The Findhorn Garden*. New York: HarperCollins, 1975.

Fizzotti, Luigi, *Il segreto di Teresa*. Ed. Eco, S. Gabriela, 1980.

Gandhi, Mahatma, *Gandhi commenta la Bhagavad Gita*. Rome: Edizioni Mediterranee, 1987.

Giovanni, Paola II, *Gli angeli. Catechesi al popolo di Dio*. Ed. Michael, Monte S. Agelo.

Giovetti, Paola, *Qualcuno è tornato*. Rome: Armenia Editore, 1981 and 1988.

_____. *Teresa Neumann di Konnersreuth*. Ed. Paoline, 1989.

Goethe, Johann Wolfgang, *Faust*, tr. Charles E. Passage. New York: Bobbs-Merrill, 1965.

Graham, Billy, *Angels*. New York: Pocket Books, 1977.

Greenberg, Martin, tr., *The Diaries of Franz Kafka 1914–1923*. London: Secher and Warburg, 1949; London: Minerva, 1992.

Jaffé, Aniela, *Apparitions and Precognition: A Study from the Point of View of C. G. Jung's Analytical Psychology*. New Hyde Park, NY: University Books, 1963.

Jaynes, Julian, *The Origin of Consciousness in the Breakdown of the Bicameral Mind*. Boston: Houghton Mifflin, 1976.

Jung, C. G., *Memories, Dreams, Reflections*. New York: Pantheon Books, 1961.

_____. *Psychological Reflections: A New Anthology of His Writings*. Princeton, NJ: Princeton University Press, 1970.

Jussek, Eugene, *Begegnung mit dem Weisen in uns: Gespraeche mit Yan Su Lu [Encounter with the Wisdom Figure in Us: Conversations with Yan Su Lu]*. Munich, Germany: Goldmann Verlag, 1986.

Luca di San Giuseppe (Padre), Santa Chiara di Monte Falco. Trevi: Tipographia Nazzarena, 1889.

Maclean, Dorothy, *To Hear the Angels Sing*. Hudson, NY: Lindisfarne Press, 1980.

Maharishi Mahesh Yogi, *Bhagavad Gita*. Rome: Edizioni Mediterranee, 1981.

Mann, Thomas, *Death in Venice*, tr. Kenneth Burke. New York: Borzoi, Alfred Knopf, 1965.

Montonati Angelo, *Le mani che guarironto la citta* (the story of Santa Francesca Romana). Ed. Paoline, 1985.

Moody, Raymond A., *Life After Life*. New York: Bantam Books; London: Corgi, 1975.

_____. *The Light Beyond*. New York: Bantam Books, 1989.

Moolenburgh, H. C., *A Handbook of Angels*. Saffron Walden, Essex, UK: C. W. Daniel, 1988.

Pasolini, Pier Paolo, *Teorema*. Milan, Italy: Garzanti Ed., 1968.

The Revised King James Version of the Holy Bible. Oxford: Oxford University Press.

Rilke, Ranier Maria, *Duinesian Elegies*, tr. Elaine E. Boney. Chapel Hill, NC: University of North Carolina Press, 1975.

Ring, Kenneth, *Heading Toward Omega: In Search of the Meaning of the Near-Death Experience*. New York: Quill, William Morrow, 1984.

Rossi, Paolo Aldo, "Il ritorno degli angeli. Gli astri e i cieli." *Prospettive nel mondo* (Rome, March, 1989), p. 153.

Rushdie, Salman, *Satanic Verses*. New York and London: Viking Penguin, 1989.

Santarelli, Giuseppe, *La Santa Casa di Loreto*. Loreto, 1988.

Shelley, Percy Bysshe, *Selected Poetry and Prose*, "Defence of Poetry." New York and London: Routledge English Texts, 1991.

Singer, June, *The Unholy Bible: A Psychological Interpretation of William Blake*, "The Marriage of Heaven and Hell." Plate 14. New York: C. G. Jung Foundation, 1970.

Sources Orientales, *Génies, Anges et Démons*. Paris: Editions du Seuil, 1971.

Spiegl, Anni, *Leben und Sterben der Therese Neumann von Konnersreuth*. Kloster Theresianum, 1976.

Steiner, Johannes, *Visionen der Theresa Neumann*. Verlag Schell & Steiner, 1979.

Steiner, Rudolf, *Spiritual Beings in the Heavenly Bodies and in the Kingdoms of Nature*. Hudson, NY: Anthroposophic Press, 1992.

_____. *The Spiritual Hierarchies and their Reflections in the Physical World: Zodiac, Planets, Cosmos*. Hudson, NY: Anthroposophic Press, 1983.

Swedenborg, Emanuel, *Heaven and Hell*. New York: American Swedenborg Printing and Publishing Society, 1859.

Tredennick, Hush, trans., *Plato: The Last Days of Socrates (Euthyphro, The Apology, Crito, Phaedo)*. New York and London: Penguin Books, 1954.

Volbden Amadeus, *Il Protettore invisibile*. Rome: Edizioni Mediterranee, 1985.